Swedish Touches

SUPERBLY SWEDISH REVISED & EXPANDED
Recipes and Traditions

edited by David Wright and Martha Wiberg Thompson

Acknowledgments

We give special thanks to Bruce Karstadt, Jan McElfish, and Curt Pederson, of The American Swedish Institute, Minneapolis; Lynne Moratzka, Harriet Johnson, and Carol Seefeldt, Gammelgården Museum, Scandia, Minnesota; Donald Myers, Barbara Booren, Stacia Seene, and Joe Lencioni, Gustavus Adolphus College, St. Peter, Minnesota; Kirby Winn, Augustana College, Rock Island, Illinois; Mike Wendel, Bishop Hill Heritage Association; Martha Downey, State of Illinois Historic Preservation Agency, Historic Sites Division, Bishop Hill; Kathy and Jim Richardson, Small World Gallery; Ron Michael, Birger Sandzén Memorial Gallery; Dean Anderson, Anderson Butik; Ann Marie Olson, Hemslöjd; and the Chamber of Commerce, all from Lindsborg, Kansas; Dana Bykowski, House of Sweden, Embassy of Sweden, Washington, D.C.; Holly Anderson, Concordia Language Village, Concordia College, Moorhead, Minnesota; Karen Jenson, Milan, Minnesota; Barry and Vivian Bergquist, Cloquet, Minnesota; Anders Neumueller, *Swedish Press,* Vancouver, Canada; Mika Roinila, Bethel College, Mishawaka, Indiana; Professor Ulf Beijbom, Swedish Emigrant Institute, Växjö, Sweden; and to all those who helped with *Superbly Swedish* and with this book.

Title-page: Rose-like flower, 1835, by Dala painter Olhans Olaf Jonsson, from *Flowers of Dalarna* by Helen Elizabeth Blanck.

Front cover: Martha Wiberg Thompson created this attractive arrangement of bread and treats for a Christmas party. Foods include Gouda, goat, Swedish Fontina, and Bond-Ost cheeses, flatbread, a tub of herring, ham, turkey, tongue, a Swedish tea ring, spritz cookies, Swedish rye bread, Christmas fruit bread, limpa bread, and a tub of butter. Christmas greens, a Dala horse, and a Swedish candle holder complete the scene.

Back cover: Jessica Greupner is standing with a straw Christmas goat (*julbock*) by an old-fashioned tree at The American Swedish Institute, Minneapolis. She is wearing a dress called *gulkolten* with a striped apron and flowered hat and scarf from Leksand in the province of Dalarna. The straw goat represents Lucifer in disguise. He was conquered by Saint Nicholas and forced to help distribute gifts to children.

ISBN 1-932043-53-5   Library of Congress Control Number: 2006932378
©2006 Penfield Books   Printed in U.S.A.

Contents

Detail from a design by Karen Jenson

Our Special Contributors

Edited by David Wright and Martha Wiberg Thompson
Associate editors: Dwayne Bourret, Joan Liffring-Zug Bourret,
Melinda Bradnan, Dorothy Crum, Connie Schnoebelen, and Jeanne L. Wright
Photography: Joan Liffring-Zug Bourret, unless otherwise credited
Graphic design: Molly Cook, MA Cook Design

In my northern Minnesota childhood, I loved visiting our Swedish-American neighbor, Hilma Lindquist, where every dinner was a smorgasbord. This cheerful optimist epitomized the Swedish people: gentle, caring, and giving, always full of hope. Penfield's first Swedish title was edited in 1983 by the late Martha Wiberg Thompson, one of 34 members of her family to attend Gustavus Adolphus College in St. Peter, Minnesota. A devout Lutheran, she was a music teacher and a community volunteer. Like mother, like daughter: Sarah Thompson Baird in Baton Rouge, Louisiana, assisted Hurricane Katrina victims. David Wright, our editor from Decorah, Iowa, lived for 27 years in New York, where he was the registrar and archivist of the Morgan Library and historian for J.P. Morgan & Co. David and his wife, Jeanne, included great Swedish artists in this book. Among them is John F. Carlson, whose winter painting was in the collection of my grandfather. Images of sculpture at Gustavus Adolphus came from Joe Lencioni, artist, web-designer, and published photographer.

Award-winning photographer Jim Richardson contributed beautiful photographs. He grew up on a Kansas farm and, although not of Swedish descent, Jim and his wife Kathy chose to raise their son in Lindsborg, Kansas, where they partake in Swedish folk dancing. We have included Karen Jenson's designs and folk art paintings. She is one of the most accomplished decorative folk painters in America. Her painting has been described as having "great freedom, vitality, and lyricism." Honorary Consul General of Sweden in Vancouver, British Columbia, Anders Neumueller contributed two delightful essays. He edits *Swedish Press*, the only English monthly publication with news from Sweden and *Scandinavian Press*, a quarterly, with news from all the Nordic countries. Anders provided the link to Prof. Mika Roinila for an essay about Canadian Swedes. With a PhD from the University of Saskatchewan, Prof. Roinila teaches geography and international studies at Bethel College, Mishawaka, Indiana. Charlotte Anderson, Lindsborg, and Kerstin Van Gilder, Iowa City, both native Swedes, contributed essays and recipes.

— Joan Liffring-Zug Bourret, publisher

Sweden and America

by David Wright

It is hard to imagine modern America without the influence of the Swedish immigrants, just as modern Sweden would have been different without impulses and innovations from America. This is our common heritage of the fantastic immigration era, a heritage which forever links our two countries. The emigration divided the Swedish people into two branches, one in Sweden and one in America. About one-fifth of all Swedes lived in America at the beginning of the twentieth century. It is an estimate that there are as many Americans of Swedish descent today as there are inhabitants in Sweden...

— Swedish historian Ulf Beijbom

In this book, we offer a glimpse into the lives of Swedish Americans, their customs and institutions, and the full calendar of their celebrations that serve to perpetuate the best of Sweden's old world traditions here in America.

The third largest country in Western Europe, Sweden occupies a land mass about ten percent greater than California. Sweden's northernmost border, well above the Arctic Circle, is about one thousand miles distant from its southern shores on the Baltic Sea. The southern tip of Sweden is about as far north as the southernmost part of Alaska.

In the late first century A.D., the Roman historian Tacitus first mentioned the "Suiones" as the inhabitants of what we now call Sweden. "Svealand" and its dwellers, the "Svear," were the country's later names, supported by linguistics and based on early medieval sources, such as the *Sagas*. In Old English and Old Norse, Svealand and Sweden were used interchangeably. The Swedish name for Sweden is *Sverige*, derived from *Svea rike*, meaning "realm of the Swedes."

Populated by nine million people, Sweden is today a constitutional monarchy with a representative democracy based on the parliamentary system. Stockholm, the capital, is home to nearly 1.5 million people; the rest of the country is sparsely populated. A prime minister and cabinet are formed by the largest party or coalition of parties. The parliament, or *Riksdag*, is a 349-member assembly.

Among the most progressive of European monarchies, Sweden passed a constitutional amendment in 1980 extending the right of royal succession to the throne for first-born females.

Sweden's famous policy of neutrality in armed conflicts originated in the early nineteenth century as a result of disastrous involvement in the Napoleonic Wars. Despite this history, Sweden voted to join the European Union in 1995. Sweden is now a strong voice in the EU for long-term sustainable economic, social, and ecological development. Despite EU membership, the Swedish currency remains the *krona*.

During the twentieth century, Sweden created the world's most generous social welfare system, providing basic economic security. Now, with economic growth slowing, Sweden's welfare state is under heavy pressure.

In a country with social welfare, it might seem strange that Sweden's aristocracy has long been a powerful force. In the Middle Ages, Sweden's king was elected by members of a council of aristocrats; the throne was not inherited. Only in the sixteenth century did the monarchy become based on familial inheritance. Swedish nobility is still organized into three classes, which have been in existence since 1561: count *(greve)*, baron *(friherre)*, and untitled nobility. Swedish dukes *(hertig)* are also counted among its royalty. Since 1902, Sweden has not granted hereditary titles or honors; in 2003, a new law abolished some privileges of the nobility.

During the seventeenth century, Sweden was a leading European nation; the king's power became absolute. After the Napoleonic Wars, lacking an heir in the established royal line, French marshal Jean-Baptiste Bernadotte became successor to the Swedish throne in 1810. The current monarch, Carl XVI Gustaf, descended from Bernadotte, is also third cousin to Queen Elizabeth II, both having descended from Britain's Queen Victoria. Sweden's heir to the throne is the King's eldest child, Victoria. She will become Sweden's first female head of state within the Bernadotte dynasty.

In the modern era, Sweden is famous for her diplomats, scientists, writers, designers, singers, and sports figures. Leading the world in the skill and depth of their writing, directing, and performing, the Swedes make major contributions to the dramatic arts. Swedes excel in the fields of design, fashion, pop music, and gastronomy. The famous Swedish affinity for contemporary design now includes pioneering the creation and execution of computer gaming technology. Swedish taste and sensibility have long been associated with simplicity, the appreciation of the beauty of ordinary objects, wit, and a deep affinity for the natural world.

Smorgasbord of Swedish History

> To describe the country is a task that defies the power of one who can only wield the pen.
>
> — Selma Lagerlöf

During her long history, Sweden was often at war. In the seventeenth century, as an important power in Europe, Sweden occupied territory almost completely surrounding the Baltic Sea. But, since 1814 and the end of the Napoleonic Wars, Sweden has lived in peace. The twentieth century saw the country's transformation from an agrarian to an industrial economy, and Swedes are known today for their remarkable entrepreneurial spirit.

Prehistory, and Earliest History, 6000 B.C. to A.D. 800

> When men are silent, the stones bear witness.
>
> — Selma Lagerlöf

Following the last ice age, around 6000 B.C., with all of Svealand free of ice, settlements began. The first inhabitants, nomadic hunters and fishers, came via the land bridge from Denmark. Petroglyphs found in northern Sweden dating as early as 9000 B.C. depict reindeer, elk, and bears. From 2300 to 500 B.C., more detailed petroglyphs show domesticated animals, ships, warfare, and agriculture. The Bronze Age began in Sweden around 1800 B.C., marked by increased evidence of trading with Europe and the British Isles. The earliest written record of Scandinavia and the Swedes was by Roman writers in the first century A.D. Sweden's Iron Age, from 500 B.C. to A.D. 800, is marked by lively trading with other areas. In A.D. 120, the oldest surviving map showing Scandinavia was created. By the third century A.D., the Swedes began using their first alphabet with runic letters.

> *If you travel over mountain, gulf, or fjord,*
> *don't forget to put food in your pack.*
>
> — Old Norse saying

A runestone from the city of Uppsala, Sweden, was given to Minneapolis and dedicated by Mayor R.T. Rybak during the Upplandsfestivalen.

The "Viking" Age, A.D. 800 to 1050

Swedish "Vikings" traveled throughout Europe, and followed the rivers of Russia to the Black Sea, trading and raiding. A Swede, Rurik the Norseman, became ruler in Russia in 862. The term "Viking" was not invented until the eleventh century. These early Swedish "Norsemen" were known as Danes, a name that dates back to A.D. 901.

> **A furore normannorum libera nos domine.**
> **"Oh lord, save us from the rage of the Nordic people."**
> — prayer in French churches during the ninth century

The richness of Nordic mythology and its pantheistic religion are well-known. The stories of Odin, Thor, Loke, and the castle Valhalla in Asgård are filled with fantastic adventures of gods, giants, elves, and dwarfs. In A.D. 829, St. Ansgar, a German bishop, introduced Christianity to Sweden in Birka, which became the first recorded outpost for Christianity in Scandinavia. Other cities were Christianized between A.D. 950 and 1030, with Sweden's conversion completed in the twelfth century. In 1008, Olof Skötkonung, elected as the first King of Sweden, accepted Christianity.

The Middle Ages, A.D. 1050 to 1520

**Perfect wisdom and power are with God,
and therefore it is established that none can prevail against it.**
— Sweden's St. Birgitta, *Celestial Revelations*

During the Swedish Middle Ages, when the king was elected by a council of aristocrats, Sweden suffered with struggles between powerful families and factions. Swedes formed towns and codified laws. They established Stockholm, a new trade center, in the thirteenth century. The Black Plague swept Sweden in the fourteenth century, killing almost one-third of the population. In 1397, the Nordic countries were unified under the Kalmar Union, an effort to counteract the economic power of the German Hanseatic League. Birgitta, founder of the Bridgettine order, was the most celebrated saint of the north, and author of extensive revelations that were widely read and admired throughout Europe.

The Vasa Period, 1520–1611

One does not have peace longer than one's neighbor wants.
— Gustav Vasa

Leading an army, Gustav Vasa defeated the Danes and became King of Sweden on June 6, 1523. This established Sweden as a free country, and the national day of June 6th recently became a public holiday in Sweden. Under Vasa's rule, Sweden became a national state with strong central authority and an absolute monarch. Although he was considered ruthless, Vasa's authority and power were crucial, and he is known as Sweden's founding father. Vasa converted himself and Sweden to Protestantism and transferred the wealth of the church to the crown. In 1541, the *Bible* was first printed in Swedish, in an edition called *Vasa's Bible*. This publication became a milestone in the development of the Swedish language and the education of the public. After his death in 1560, his three sons carried on his policies. Vasa's role in Swedish history endures. At the end of the nineteenth century, Strindberg wrote his famous *Vasa Trilogy*, and entitled one of the plays, *Gustav Vasa*.

Gustavus Adolphus, 1611–1632

dominum maris baltic
"supremacy of the Baltic Sea"

*Gustavus Adolphus (1594–1632) depicted in an "Old Gus" statue,
Gustavus Adolphus College, St. Peter, Minnesota*

The brilliant grandson of Gustav Vasa, Gustav II Adolf, was more famous by the Latinized version of his name, Gustavus Adolphus. One of the best-known kings in Swedish history, Gustavus Adolphus was a political genius and master of warfare strategy. Marked by constant war, his reign included participation in the Thirty Years War, beginning in 1630. Under his leadership, Sweden established itself as a great power in Europe and expanded its rule to include Finland, the Baltic States, and a large part of Germany. This was also the age of universities, town planning, and major trade, with important iron and copper exports. Gustavus Adolphus, the "Lion of the North," died in battle in 1632. A few years later, in 1638, the first Swedish immigrants to America established New Sweden.

Right: *The first Swedes and Finns from the* Kalmar Nyckel *landed on the rocks, a natural wharf, in Wilmington, Delaware. They named their fort in honor of Queen Christina.*

Christina, Queen of Sweden, 1632–1654

...this girl shall become as good as any boy.

— Gustavus Adolphus

King Gustavus Adolphus said these words, knowing that his only surviving child, Christina, would become heir to the Swedish throne. This daughter was six years old when her father died in battle; she came of age and began her rule in 1644. During her lifetime, Christina exceeded even the fame of Elizabeth I of Britain. She is remembered for her patronage of the arts and literary culture. Christina was well-educated and had a facility for languages. She drew attention for her refusal to accept the traditional feminine role and was educated as a prince. She invited musicians, artists, and writers to Sweden, including the French philosopher Descartes, who became her tutor. In 1654, Christina shocked the world by abdicating her throne and converting to Catholicism. Spending the rest of her life in Rome, she became a powerful influence on the Papacy, and is one of only four women buried in St. Peter's. Christina's dramatic life has inspired numerous books and plays, including Strindberg's play in 1901, and the famous biographical film of 1933, which was a vehicle for another Swede, Greta Garbo.

Photo, The American Swedish Historical Museum, Philadelphia

The Establishment of Civilization in the Delaware Valley
This ceiling painting by Christian von Schneidau is in the Grand Hall at The American Swedish Historical Museum, Philadelphia.

Karl XII, Spartan Warrior-King, 1697–1718

It is said that God is always on the side of the heaviest battalions.

— Voltaire

Karl XII (also known as Charles XII) was a charismatic leader and great general, one of history's most brilliant tacticians. Threatened by the anti-Swedish alliance of Russia, Poland, and Denmark, Karl XII defeated these powers, most memorably with a brilliant victory at Narva against Russia in 1700. Following treaties in 1706, Sweden briefly became the predominant military power in Northern Europe.

Victory was followed by miscalculation, and the Swedish forces were badly defeated in 1709 during an invasion of Russia. Karl XII's death in battle in 1718 marked the end of the Swedish empire. In 1731, Voltaire published his *History of Charles XII*, which remains one of the classics of biographical art.

The Era of Liberty and Enlightenment, 1718–1771

Here everyone is behaving like flies that have survived the winter and come to life again...

— from a letter describing Stockholm in 1718

After Christina's abdication in 1654, Sweden's autocratic rulers persisted in warfare and absolutism. An important military defeat in Russia in 1709 brought an end to the expansion of the Swedish state, leaving only Finland and minor Baltic territory under her rule. A new constitution of 1719–1720 placed power in the hands of the *Riksdag*, Sweden's parliament. The European Enlightenment inspired the advancement of science and philosophy in Sweden; this period laid the foundation for Sweden's later heritage of freedom. A great era in Sweden's history, the eighteenth century produced impressive economic, scientific, and cultural advancements.

Gustavian wallpaper design from Swedish Folkart *by Diane Edwards*

The Gustavian Age, 1771–1809

**...the singer found his note, and life was young,
Gustavian all Swedish things became.**
— Esaias Tegnér, the father of modern poetry in Sweden

One of Sweden's most captivating rulers, Gustav III, came to the throne in 1771. An ardent Francophile, he became one of Europe's most enlightened monarchs. Under his rule there was gradual and more equal distribution of rights and privileges, and the elimination of trade restrictions. In 1782, special regulations permitted Jews to settle in Swedish cities. In 1783, Sweden signed a treaty with the new country called the United States of America, becoming the first neutral country in Europe to recognize the new republic. In 1786, Gustav III founded the Swedish Academy (*Svenska Akademien*) to further the "purity, vigor, and majesty" of the Swedish language. Sweden now experienced a great flowering of its own culture with great works by poets, painters, sculptors, and architects.

Elegant manor houses, beautiful silver, and distinctive furniture are a part of the Gustavian Age; this period is now called the golden age of Swedish decorative arts. Gustav III loved the theatre, writing plays and participating in productions. He wrote the well-known opera called "Gustav Wasa." In 1792, a fanatic group of Swedish noblemen, who resented the growing loss of their influence, assassinated Gustav III.

Emigration and Industrialization, 1809–1905

Death to all Kings!

— a tattoo on the arm of Jean-Baptiste Bernadotte,
later King Karl XIV Johan of Sweden

Alliances during the Napoleonic Wars proved disastrous and cost Sweden much political clout, a well as its influence in Russia and Finland. The Swedish King had no heir; Francophile Swedes in 1810 elected one of Napoleon's generals, Jean-Baptiste Bernadotte, as Crown Prince, with the hope that this alliance might help Sweden regain Finland. In 1812, Denmark relinquished control of Norway to Sweden. Although the Norwegians drew up their own constitution, they were forced into the union with Sweden in 1814. From 1818 until his death in 1844, Bernadotte became King Karl XIV Johan of Sweden, establishing the Bernadotte dynasty, a new order of succession and the forerunner of today's monarchy.

Between 1840 and 1900, over 850,000 Swedes emigrated, mainly to North America. This same period saw a large increase in Sweden's population. With industrial advancements, and with religious, labor, liberal, and temperance movements, Sweden was changing. Compulsory education was introduced, along with a more parliamentarian form of government. Norway unilaterally declared its union with Sweden dissolved in 1905, and negotiations resulted in a split of the two countries without bloodshed.

The Twentieth Century: Neutrality and Solidarity

**In our era, the road to holiness necessarily passes
through the world of action.**
— Dag Hammarskjöld
Swedish diplomat and Secretary-General of the United Nations,
1953–1961

Sweden's economy was vibrant in the twentieth century due to worldwide demand for her commodities, including: steel, wood pulp, matches, ball-bearings, telephones, autos, and vacuum cleaners. Industrialization brought more than fifty percent of the Swedish population into urban areas. Sweden witnessed a growing role of the State and the shrinking power of its monarch, changing into a modern welfare state with emphasis on a growing democracy. In 1909, all men became eligible to vote; all Swedish women gained the vote in 1919, one year before that right was extended to American women. Sweden joined the League of Nations, but remained officially neutral in both world wars, becoming, in the 1940s, an important destination for refugees, especially from Norway and Denmark.

The second half of the century increased public expenditure and redistributed taxation. Sweden adopted a new constitution in 1974; its major provision was "all power derives from the people." With one of the world's highest standards of living and admirable literacy, Sweden also gained world status as a peacemaker and humanitarian force. Prime Minister Olof Palme, with a profound commitment to the elimination of apartheid in South Africa, was assassinated in 1986. His murder was the first act of its kind in modern Swedish history and produced an impact in Scandinavia similar to the shock in America after John Kennedy's death in 1963.

För Sverige-i tiden
"For Sweden — with the times"
— the motto of H.M. Carl XVI Gustaf

Sweden's Future in the Twenty-first Century

**We in Sweden must develop a new definition of welfare,
less materialistic — one that stresses culture.**
— Margot Wallström, Swedish politician and diplomat

The challenges of Sweden's future are formidable. With high unemployment and an influx of immigrants from Africa, the Middle East, and the Balkans, Sweden is struggling to maintain its high standard of living. More than ten percent of Sweden's population is made up of immigrants or the children of immigrants. With its new role in the European Union, Sweden is moving away from neutrality to integration with the rest of Europe. Along with this European union and the modern global economy, Sweden is experiencing an enhanced appreciation, even a nostalgia, for its own language, literature, and cultural tradition.

Swedes in North America

**Sweden is the home of my ancestors
and I have reserved a special place in my heart for Sweden.**
— Carl D. Anderson (1905–1991)
Swedish-American recipient of the Nobel Prize for Physics, 1936

Emigration: The View from Sweden

Peace, vaccination, and potatoes
(reasons most often given for the increase in Swedish population during
the nineteenth century that resulted in massive emigration)

Swedish settlement in America is almost as old as any European colonial presence on this continent. During the period of its greatest power and expansion, Sweden chartered The New Sweden Company. In 1638, just eighteen years after the arrival of the *Mayflower* in Massachusetts, the first Swedes arrived at a spot near Wilmington, Delaware. They created *Nya Sverige* (New Sweden), the first permanent European settlement in the Delaware Valley. Soon this colony was joined by settlers from twelve more Swedish expeditions. The major period of Swedish emigration took place from the mid-1840s until 1930 when nearly twenty percent of Sweden's population emigrated. Just before World War I, one-fifth of all living Swedes were in North America.

In 1965, the Swedish Emigrant Institute (*Svenska Emigrantinstitutet*) was founded in Växjö in the province of Småland in southcentral Sweden. The Institute preserves records, interviews, and artifacts from the period of major Swedish emigration. A permanent exhibition, "The Dream of America," displays pictures, models, artifacts, and recordings that explain Swedish emigration. The Institute now documents the emigrant experience from another perspective — for those who have recently come to Sweden from their homes in other lands.

Immigration: *Svenskamerika* (Swedish America)

Don't throw away the old bucket
until you know whether the new one will hold water.
— Swedish proverb

Most Swedish immigrants, beginning in the mid-1840s, settled in Midwestern states where land grants were then being issued. Western Illinois, western Wisconsin, Iowa, and Minnesota were the earliest destinations; after the Civil War, Swedes settled further west in Kansas and Nebraska. About fifteen percent chose areas in New England and New York; ten percent ended up on the West Coast, primarily in Washington state and California. The highest number of Swedes, however, settled in Minnesota and Illinois. Minnesota had the highest percentage of Swedish population; Chicago became the Swedish-American capital. During the early twentieth century, only Stockholm, Sweden, was home to more Swedish-born people than Chicago. Swedish inspired place names of American towns reflect these settlements. There are nine states with towns or townships named "Stockholm": Iowa, Kentucky, Maine, Minnesota, New Jersey, New York, South Dakota, Texas, and Wisconsin. Runners-up include eight states with towns named "Sweden," and seven states with towns named "Mora." There are also towns named "Malmo," "Swedesburg," "New Sweden," and "Upsala" in Iowa, Maine, Minnesota, Nebraska, North Carolina, Pennsylvania, and Texas.

In 1981, the Swenson Swedish Immigration Research Center at Augustana College, Rock Island, Illinois, became a national archives, library, and research center, and has been called "a gold mine of Swedish immigrant history." Its resources are available by appointment. Many visitors consult these records for family history and genealogical research. The Center holds conferences, awards fellowships, creates publications, and promotes new research — all in the field of Swedish-American studies.

Swedes in Canada

by Mika Roinila, PhD

The best place to find a helping hand is at the end of your own arm.
— Swedish proverb

Swedes began to arrive in Canada in the beginning of the nineteenth century. The first Swede in Canada was Jacob Fahlstrom. Born in Stockholm in 1793, Fahlstrom arrived at the mouth of the York River on Hudson Bay in 1807. Working for the Hudson's Bay Company in 1809, he later settled along the Red River at the Selkirk Settlement in 1812 as the only Swede. Many of the earliest Swedes who followed left Canada for the United States; but, as farmland became less available in the U.S. after the 1850s, Swedes came to Canada.

In addition to farming, many Swedes worked as miners and lumberjacks in Northern Ontario, or as laborers on the Canadian Pacific Railway. In 1885, the completed railway opened Canadian prairies, and Winnipeg became the center of Swedish immigration in Canada. Winnipeg became a virtual Swedish colony; the Swedish language was dominant until the 1920s. In western Manitoba, a settlement near Erickson was founded in 1886 and still retains its Swedish presence. In Saskatchewan, rural Swedish colonies include the New Stockholm Colony, founded in 1885. The Augustana Synod established the first of Canada's Swedish-Lutheran congregations in New Stockholm in 1889.

The first Swedes in Alberta established homesteads at Bittern Lake near Wetaskiwin in 1892. Bittern Lake soon formed the nucleus of a large concentration of Swedish settlements in the area. First were farmers who had emigrated from the United States; then, after 1900, an increasing number arrived directly from Sweden. They were a diverse group: some were industrial workers, others were engineers or businessmen involved in the export industries, drawn west by emerging opportunities in the prairies. Swedish Canadians involved in railway building and logging came to British Columbia. While Edmonton has the highest percentage of Swedish Canadians in its population, Vancouver has maintained its ranking as the most populous Swedish-Canadian center. Finland-Swedes (native-born Finns with Swedish mother tongue) are also found in the Vancouver area. According to the 2001 Canadian Census, nearly 300,000 Canadians claimed Swedish descent. Most Swedes were found in British Columbia, Alberta

(79,000), and Ontario (55,000). The highest urban populations included Vancouver, Edmonton, Calgary, Toronto, and Winnipeg. Swedes in Canada have published a number of periodicals in cities such as Winnipeg, Toronto, and Vancouver. The longest-running Swedish periodical was the weekly *Canadian-Tidningen,* founded in 1892. It merged with the *Swedish-American Tribune* of Chicago in 1970. *The Finland-Swedish Canada Svensken* appeared in Toronto between 1961–1978. Today, *Swedish Press* is North America's only Swedish monthly magazine. Published in Vancouver, it has worldwide distribution.

The Vasa Order and Vasa Lodges have played an important part in the preservation of Swedish traditions in Canada. Founded in 1896, this Swedish-American fraternal organization now has nearly 300 lodges in the Vasa Order, and district lodges in the U.S., Sweden, and Canada. Named after King Gustav Vasa — the first king of modern Sweden — it welcomes members of Scandinavian descent. There are many Vasa parks in Canada and the U.S., where the lodges organize events, including Midsummer observances.

Swedish-Canadian cultural organizations are often affiliated with pan-Scandinavian associations. Many of these groups establish events and participate in annual festivals. Advertised as the best multicultural festival in the world, *Winnipeg's Folklorama* has included the Swedish Canadians in its Scandinavian Pavilion. An active SWEA (Swedish Women's Education Association) meets in cities such as Vancouver and Toronto, and organizes fairs and other events. The Swedish Embassy in Ottawa organizes events across the country and distributes information about Canadian-Swedish events on its website. Swedish Canadians have contributed much to cooperatives, credit unions, and unions. Canadians of Swedish origin eventually were drawn into Canadian politics as well. The Swedish Liberal Club of Winnipeg, founded in 1908, encouraged many to become naturalized and to take full advantage of their rights as citizens. Perhaps the highest political office reached by a Swedish Canadian was Alberta-born Harry Simon, Premier of Alberta from 1968 to 1971. Other well-known Canadians of Swedish descent include broadcaster Pamela Wallin, Judge Tom Berger, architect Arthur Erickson, and poet Ralph Gustafson. The Lakehead Social History Institute in Thunder Bay is assisting Elinor Barr in a major research project to document Swedish immigration to Canada and to establish a record of the impact Swedes and their descendants have made in Canada.

Swedes in the United States

Selected sites, settlements, organizations, and festivals
from Maine to California
What is hidden in snow comes forth in the thaw.

— Swedish proverb

New England: Maine's Swedish Colony
Not far from the Canadian border, Maine's historic Swedish Colony includes the towns of New Sweden, Stockholm, and several surrounding villages. Founded in 1870 by Swedish settlers who were drawn to Aroostook County in northern Maine by the state legislature's promise of land, these towns preserve their heritage with several historic societies, museums, and festivals. Most famous is the annual two-day *Midsommar* Festival held in New Sweden every mid-June. This area is also the birthplace of Nordic (cross-country) skiing, brought here by the original Swedish settlers.

Massachusetts: Greater Boston Area
Boston's Swedish Consulate serves all New England. The Swedish-American Chamber of Commerce of New England, located in nearby Waltham, encourages cultural and commercial ties. Also in Boston is the Swedish Women's Education Association, which helps preserve the Swedish language in America and spreads interest in Swedish culture and tradition. The Swedish Charitable Society of Greater Boston, the Swedish Home in West Newton, and the *Swedish Heritage Press* in Norwell are all well-known. Boston's Museum of Fine Arts contains one of the best collections of paintings by Swedish artist Anders Zorn (1860–1920), one of the most popular portrait artists of his day.

Massachusetts: Greater Brockton
The earliest Swedish immigrants arrived in Brockton around 1844 and established a strong presence on Cape Cod and south of Boston. Brockton became a stopping-off point for Swedes on the way to the Midwest.

Massachusetts: Worcester
In 1920, Worcester's Swedish population was the country's third largest, after Minneapolis and Chicago. New England's industrial expansion drew thousands of Swedes to this city. Worcester became the center of Swedish language publications in America. The magazine *SVEA,* originally published here since

1898, was purchased in 1966 by the *Nordstjernan* newspaper in Brooklyn. Worcester is home to the Swedish National Federation, an umbrella organization, which plans an annual *Midsommar* festival in Shrewsbury and a Lucia pageant each December. The Swedish Ancestry Research Association (SARA) has served New England since 1994. The Nordic Heritage Trust of New England is located in nearby Charlton.

All beginnings are difficult.
— Swedish proverb

Mid-Atlantic: Delaware Valley

At the height of its colonizing period, Sweden sent an organized group of settlers to establish a colony under the Swedish crown. In 1638, two ships reached Delaware Bay. The colonists constructed a fort near present-day Wilmington, and named it Fort Christina, creating the first permanent European settlement in the Delaware Valley. By 1713, growing Dutch and English influence prevailed. One enduring legacy of the Swedish/Finnish settlement was the first use of the log house, which became the standard structure of American immigrant frontier life.

Holy Trinity (Old Swedes) Church, Wilmington, Delaware

Since 2000, visitors enjoy Wilmington's New Sweden Centre, an interpretive and hands-on center for colonial history in the Delaware Valley. Nearby stands Holy Trinity (Old Swedes) Church, built in 1698, and the oldest church in America in continuous use. Next to the church stands the restored Hendrickson house from 1690, one of the oldest houses in the country. Visitors also enjoy Fort Christina Park; the Stallcop log cabin; and the *Kalmar Nyckel* shipyard, replica, and monument. The Delaware Swedish Colonial Society organizes annual events: each March a commemoration of the 1638 landing, a *Midsommar* festival in June, and a mid-December Lucia pageant in the Old Swedes Church.

New Jersey

Opened in 1988 by King Carl XVI Gustaf, Bridgeton's New Sweden Farmstead Museum is a replica of a seventeenth-century farm. This complex near Wilmington has several buildings and original artifacts, some on loan from Sweden. Stanhope's Waterloo Village holds *ScanFest* each year on the Labor Day weekend. In late June, Hackettstown celebrates Midsummer in Vasa Park. From 1893 to 1995, East Orange was the home of Upsala College, one of only a handful of Swedish-American institutions of higher learning. Despite an offer of loans from its four sister colleges in the Midwest, Upsala closed in 1995.

Midway between Philadelphia and Wilmington, in southwestern New Jersey, Swedesboro is home to the beautiful Old Swedes Trinity Church. Built in 1784, the church is recently restored. In nearby Gibbstown stands the Nothnagel Cabin, the oldest log structure surviving in the western hemisphere. Built soon after the Swedes arrived in 1698, the log house is privately owned and can be visited free by advance telephone appointment.

Gloria Dei Church, Philadelphia, where Jenny Lind sang, and Carl Milles donated a Swedish chandelier and two model ships.

Pennsylvania

The American Swedish Historical Museum in South Philadelphia, founded in 1926, is the oldest Swedish museum in the country. Visitors enjoy a Swedish farmhouse, displays about famous Swedes, examples of Swedish glass, and works by Swedish artists. The Museum organizes an annual Midsummer Celebration each June.

The American Swedish Historical Museum, Philadelphia, is modeled after a seventeenth-century Swedish manor house, Eriksberg Castle, Södermanland. The museum was founded in 1926.

The Swedish Colonial Society, West Chester, founded in 1909 and dedicated to preserving the legacy of the New Sweden Colony, is the oldest Swedish historical organization in the U.S. The Society established Governor Printz Park, on Tinicum Island near Philadelphia's airport, in 1938.

New York
Although pan-Scandinavian in its mission, The American-Scandinavian Foundation, with headquarters in Scandinavia House on Park Avenue in Manhattan, is an important cultural center for Swedish Americans. The Swedish-American Chamber of Commerce, founded in 1906 in New York, is the oldest organization of its kind in America. *Nordstjernan*, the oldest and largest Swedish-American newspaper still published, serves the entire country. New York is also home to the Swedish Tourist Board and the Swedish Folkdancers of New York, a group in existence for over one hundred years. The Consulate General of Sweden in New York and the Swedish Information Service organize an annual Midsummer festival in Battery Park City. Swedish language services are held in the Church of Sweden (*Svenska Kyrkan*), located since 1978 on East 48th Street in Manhattan.

District of Columbia: Washington, D.C., and surrounding area
Sweden has captured the attention of the world with the construction in Georgetown of an embassy and trade center called the House of Sweden, located on the shores of the Potomac. The Sveaborg Society, promoting Swedish holidays and traditions, serves Baltimore and nearby areas. The Augustana Lutheran Church in Washington (*Svenska Kyrkan i DC*) holds services in Swedish on the first Sunday of each month.

I am Swedish. My father and mother came from Sweden. I wondered if the Germans, Italians, and Polish...felt a call of blood like that.

— Carl Sandburg (1878–1967)
author, poet, citizen of Illinois

Illinois: Chicago

"The Swedes built Chicago" is a well-known saying in the Midwest. Before the famous fire of 1871, Chicago's near-northside contained Swedetown with its Swedish Snuff Street. Swedetown was surpassed by the development farther north of Andersonville, home to the huge number of Swedish immigrants arriving after the 1880s. Chicago was the capital center for Swedish Americans, with a greater Swedish population by 1900 than lived in Sweden's second largest city. In these years, it was possible to live in Chicago without speaking any language but Swedish. In 1857, the Swedish immigrants founded their first social club here, quickly followed by other associations, churches, fraternal orders, and professional groups.

Today Chicago remains an important center for several Swedish-American institutions, including the Swedish-American Museum Center, located in Andersonville on the northside. Founded in 1976 and in its current location since 1987, the Museum Center features a children's museum of immigration, a special hands-on, interactive installation for ages three to twelve. Celebrating all the Swedish festivals, the Museum Center is particularly known for its Midsummer Celebration in mid-June, one of the great neighborhood festivals in Chicago. The Swedish-American Historical Society sponsors, publishes, and sells books and a membership journal all about the history and meaning of the Swedish in America. North Park University, founded by Swedish immigrants in 1891, is in northwest Chicago; its Center for Scandinavian Studies has initiated a Midsummer Festival, holds a *Sankta Lucia* pageant, and administers the Archives of The Swedish-American Historical Society. Also in Chicago are the Central Swedish Committee, an umbrella group serving Swedish institutions and businesses in northern Illinois; and the Raoul Wallenberg Humanitarian Institute, an educational non-profit group perpetuating the legacy of Raoul Wallenberg, the Swedish hero who rescued thousands of refugees during World War II.

Illinois: Geneva

Geneva's Swedish Days, the last week each June, has been called "the granddaddy of Illinois festivals." This six-day festival has been held each year since 1949.

Illinois: Rockford
The Swedish Historical Society of Rockford operates the renovated Erlander House Museum. Built by a Swedish family in 1871, the house is the center of cultural programs that promote Rockford's Swedish-American heritage. Special events include *Midsommar's Dag* in June and a Lucia Fest in early December.

Illinois: Galesburg
Popular with Swedish immigrants, Galesburg originated *Hemlandet*, the first Swedish-language newspaper in the U.S. Galesburg's most famous son, the Pulitzer-prize winning poet and Lincoln biographer, Carl Sandburg, was born here in 1878. Today his birthplace is a historic site; the house is open to the public, along with a garden and Sandburg's nearby gravesite.

> **For the land we have taken is large and wide, and is such as none of us realized was to be found in the world.**
> — Pehr Jansson of Bishop Hill, Illinois
> letter to his brother in Sweden, 1846

Illinois: Bishop Hill
The Bishop Hill Colony in western Illinois was a utopian community founded in 1846 by religious pietist Eric Jansson and his followers. Named after Jansson's birthplace, *Biskops Kulla* in Sweden, Bishop Hill was a significant force in Swedish immigration to the United States. From 1846 to 1861, this "utopia on the prairie" attracted over one thousand Swedish immigrants, who erected twenty large buildings for communal use. In 1850, Jansson's murder shattered the colony's religious unity. Leadership passed to a seven-member board. Charges of financial mismanagement led to the dissolution of the Colony in 1861, with the distribution of communal property.

Today Bishop Hill is a tiny village with a living heritage. Through the combined efforts of Heritage Association, State of Illinois Historic Preservation Agency, Old Settlers' Association, Village Board, Arts Council, and private citizens, thirteen of the original buildings have been restored and preserved. Visitors delight in touring the impressive 1854 Steeple Building, the 1848 Colony Church, and many other smaller historic places. A new structure, the Bishop Hill Museum, contains the remarkable record of Bishop Hill Colony life painted by Olof Krans, one of America's foremost folk artists. Many visitors pursue genealogical research at the Vasa Order of America's Archives.

Special celebrations at Bishop Hill include Midsummer Festival in June, Old Settlers' Days in September, *Jordbruksdagarna* (Agriculture Days) in late

September, *Julmarknad* (Christmas market) on Thanksgiving weekend, Lucia nights in December, and the early *Julotta* service on Christmas morning. Many craft workshops and cultural events are also held throughout the year.

Bishop Hill's historic Colony Church (1848) seated one thousand worshippers in handmade pews of native walnut. During Colony years, services were held several times each day. See pages 46–47 for more photographs from the Bishop Hill Heritage Association.

Illinois: Andover
On the prairie midway between Rock Island and Galesburg, is the tiny Jenny Lind Chapel, the mother church for the Augustana Lutheran Synod. Built between 1850 and 1854, construction was interrupted by a cholera epidemic that killed many Swedish settlers. Their gravestones stand nearby. The Chapel is named after the world-renowned Swedish singer who donated $1,500 for its construction; but Jenny Lind, "the Swedish Nightingale," never visited the Chapel.

Jenny Lind (in La Sonnambula*), an engraving by W. H. Mote after a painting by J. W. Wright*

The Jenny Lind Chapel, Andover, Illinois, built in the midst of an epidemic, was first pressed into service as a hospital; lumber intended for its steeple had to be used for coffins.

Illinois: Rock Island

Rock Island is home to Augustana College, America's oldest college founded by Swedish immigrants. Established in 1860 in Chicago, the college moved to its present site on a hilltop in Rock Island in 1875. Augustana's Denkmann Memorial Library includes the Swenson Swedish Immigration Research Center. Founded in 1981, this research center is the first stop for anyone interested in Swedish immigrant history.

What the sons seek to forget, the grandsons seek to remember.
— Marcus Lee Hansen, immigration historian

Iowa: Five Swedish Towns
Swedesburg is home to a Swedish-American museum of local immigration history. Celebrating Midsummer each June, Swedesburg often hosts folk dancers from Sweden. New Sweden (Jefferson County) was settled in 1845, becoming the first lasting Swedish settlement during the nineteenth century in the U.S. Stratford, in the heart of the Swedish-American area near Des Moines, is where the Stratford Historical Society has created a Swedish-American museum from an 1850s farmhouse. Nearby Boone is home to the birthplace of Mamie Doud Eisenhower (1896–1979), one of the nation's best-loved first ladies. (See page 62.) Stanton, a tiny town with a small museum in the southwest corner of the state, has been called "the Swedish capital of Iowa." Stanton became famous when it converted its watertower into the world's largest Swedish coffee pot. This landmark attracted so much attention that the town built a second watertower shaped like a coffee cup.

Wisconsin
One of the state's earliest Swedish settlements was New Uppsala, Pine Lake, in Waukesha County. A group led by Gustav Unonius, a law graduate from Uppsala University, arrived at this spot near Milwaukee in 1841. Unonius has been called "the father of Swedish immigration" because of his widely-read letters home, and for his dream to establish a cultural center on the frontier. He published an influential account of immigration, his autobiography called "A Pioneer in Northwest America," in 1861. New Uppsala was shortlived; the site is marked by a plaque.

Thirty miles west of Milwaukee, in Genesee Depot, the famous American theatrical legends Alfred Lunt and Lynn Fontanne built an estate called *Ten Chimneys*. Celebrating Lunt's Swedish heritage, the main house contains many antique Swedish stoves, folk murals, and decorations. In 1932, the Lunts imported an eighteenth-century Swedish log cabin and reassembled it near the main house, where it can be seen during tours of the estate, now open to the public by appointment. Many Swedes settled in northwestern Wisconsin, but the village of Stockholm is located on the Mississippi River about seventy miles southeast of St. Paul. Founded in the 1850s, this charming town with beautiful river views contains a small museum of local history.

This Minnesota is a glorious country, and just the country for Northern immigrants — just the country for a new Scandinavia.

— Fredrika Bremer (1801–1865)
Swedish writer and feminist activist

Minnesota

More Swedish immigrants made their home in Minnesota than any other state. Wielding an enormous influence on Minnesota's history, politics, and culture, the Swedes settled in the Twin Cities in numbers second only to Chicago.

The first Swedes reached Scandia in the 1850s; *Gammel Kyrkan*, a church built in 1856, stands on the grounds of Gammelgården Museum in Scandia. An hour north of the Twin Cities, Mora boasts the Kanabec History Center and an annual folk art festival each September. Mora is the site of Minnesota's largest annual ski race in February, the *Vasaloppet*. This long distance cross-country event covers 58 kilometers and is modeled on the famous race of the same name that concludes its course in Mora, Sweden, sister city of Mora, Minnesota. Near Chisago Lakes, Lindstrom, sister city to Tingsryd, Sweden, holds its Karl Oskar Days in early July. Named for a character in Vilhelm Moberg's classic novels of Swedish immigration to Minnesota, Karl Oskar Days are a five-day celebration of heritage.

Gustavus Adolphus College, St. Peter, Minnesota, was founded in 1862 by a Swedish immigrant Lutheran pastor. Named for the Swedish king who defended Protestantism during the Thirty Years War, the Gustavus Adolphus liberal arts curriculum includes Scandinavian studies. The Folke Bernadotte Memorial Library is dedicated to the United Nations mediator assassinated while on a peacekeeping mission in the Middle East. The Alfred Nobel Hall of Science, named for the great Swedish inventor and philanthropist, hosts the annual Nobel Conference, addressing issues in the natural and social sciences. The Jussi Björling Concert Hall is named after the internationally famous Swedish tenor.

Don't forget a trip to Alexandria, Minnesota, to see the world-famous Kensington Runestone at the Runestone Museum. Ever since a Swedish immigrant farmer discovered this curiously inscribed stone in 1898, a debate about its authenticity rages on.

Close to the geographic center of Minnesota, near Little Falls on the banks of the Mississippi River, is the Charles Lindbergh Historic Site.

Minnesota: St. Paul and Minneapolis

Attracted by work in railroads, mining, foundries, mills, breweries, and lumber yards, the Swedes in St. Paul created an enclave called Swede Hollow.

The American Swedish Institute is south of downtown Minneapolis. The Institute is housed in a thirty-three room mansion built in 1908 and donated by legendary newspaperman Swan J. Turnblad. Turnblad made his fortune and place in history as the publisher of a Swedish-language newspaper, *Svenska Amerikanska Posten*. Today's American Swedish Institute is an important museum and education center, as well as a monument to the success of the Swedish immigrant. The Institute has courses in language, folk arts, history, and culture, as well as an active children's education program. The mansion's top floor contains a semi-permanent exhibition of Swedish life in the Twin Cities featuring artifacts, as well as vintage sound and video recordings. Popular events include *Midsommar* in June and a monthly *smörgåsbord* on Sundays in the cafe. The acquisition of an adjacent property is making possible the expansion of the Institute and the creation of a Cultural and Education Center with additional space for exhibitions, classrooms, offices, collection storage, a restaurant, library, and auditorium.

The American Swedish Institute is also a center of the wider educational and diplomatic community for Swedish Americans. The Institute's President is Honorary Consul General for Sweden in the Twin Cities. Also at the Institute is the Swedish Council of America, the premier umbrella organization for all Swedish-American groups in Sweden, Canada, and the U.S. The Institute is the headquarters or meeting place of more than twenty-five clubs and organizations, including the Swedish Genealogical Society of Minnesota, the Gustavus II Adolphus Society, the Swedish-American Chamber of Commerce, and the ASI *Spelmanslag* (traditional Swedish fiddle music group).

Sjölunden ("Lake of the Woods") is the Swedish summer language program of Concordia Language Village near Bemidji, Minnesota. Members of The American Swedish Institute are eligible for scholarships for these immersion language programs for children and adults, including youth programs, teacher seminars, and Elderhostels. Also available in Minneapolis is the popular *Barndalen* ("children's valley") class, a pre-kindergarten Swedish language immersion course for ages three to five, planned and offered in partnership between the Concordia Language Village and The American Swedish Institute.

Texas

The first group of Swedish immigrants in Texas arrived in 1838. The state once had three Swedish-language newspapers, the last published until 1982. Austin had its *Svenska kullen* (Swedish hill). Texas place names indicate the widespread influence of Swedish settlers in Lund, New Sweden, West Sweden, Stockholm, and Swensondale. Houston is home to the Texas Swedish Cultural Foundation, an organization aiding higher education in the visual arts, music, and literature. Round Rock is home to the Palm House Museum & Visitor Center, the restored house of the town's founding family, with authentic furnishings and a typical Swedish-American kitchen.

> **It was good to see the Stars and Stripes side by side**
> **with the yellow and blue of the Swedish flag.**
> — Dr. Emory Lindquist
> "The Meaning of the Visit of the King of Sweden,"
> *The Bethany Magazine,* Spring 1976

Kansas: Lindsborg

"Little Sweden, U.S.A." is Lindsborg, the center of Swedish life and culture in Kansas. Settled in 1869 by Swedish immigrant pioneers, Lindsborg retains a rich Swedish heritage. The McPherson County Old Mill Museum preserves an 1898 roller mill, the Swedish pavilion from the 1904 St. Louis World's Fair (built in the style of a Swedish manor house), and several other historic buildings. The Dala horse, symbol of Swedish frugality and dexterity, is a central motif in the city's logo.

Bethany College in Lindsborg, founded by Swedish immigrants in 1881, has the Bethany Oratorio Society, one of the oldest in the nation, which sings Handel's *Messiah* annually since 1882. The Birger Sandzén Memorial Gallery, located on the south edge of the Bethany campus, contains the largest collection of paintings, prints, drawings, and watercolors by this famous Swedish-American artist who taught at the college for fifty-two years. This museum has been called "one of the most important cultural attractions in the state." The beautiful Bethany Lutheran Church, built in 1874 with an interior reminiscent of churches in rural Sweden, was the first church of the Swedish immigrants and the site of the first classes at Bethany College. *Svensk Hyllningsfest,* first held in 1941, is a biennial tribute to Swedish pioneers. Held now for three days each October of odd-numbered years, *Hyllningsfest* means "Swedish honoring festival." Participating in every festival are Lindsborg's Swedish Folk Dancers and the *Folkdanslag* (adult group). The

Bethany Midsummer's Festival features the folk dancers, along with art/craft fairs, music, and a fine smorgasbord. At Christmastime, there is a Tomte-Snowflake Parade, along with *Jultomte's* Swedish stories, a *Jultide* concert, and the Lucia Fest on the second Saturday each December.

Much like Sweden, California is very committed to energy efficiency.
— Joseph Desmond, California Undersecretary for Energy Affairs

California
Sweden and California's state government are working together to advance the use of renewable fuels through exchange of technology and ideas. California's large number of Swedish Americans draws on the services of such varied organizations as *Fröken Fredag* (a network for Swedish women working in Los Angeles) to Siliconvikings.com (an Internet resource for Swedes working in the Bay Area). There is a Swedish Folk Dance Club in Monrovia and a Swedish-American Women's Club in Glendale. In the center of California, Fresno County's Kingsburg, settled in the 1870s, calls itself the "Swedish Village." With a watertower coffeepot five hundred times larger than life, Kingsburg has Swedish architecture and atmosphere, with banners and Dala horses.

Washington: Seattle
A Swedish immigrant surgeon founded Swedish Medical Center in Seattle in 1910. Today "Swedish" (as it is known) is the largest hospital in Washington state. The Swedish Cultural Center, founded in 1882 as the Swedish Club, has a library and many programs. The Nordic Heritage Museum is pan-Scandinavian. The museum has a "Sweden Room" as a permanent exhibition, and a meeting place for the SVEA male chorus of Seattle, the Swedish Women's Chorus, and the Swedish Cultural Society, the only group whose meetings are held in the Swedish language. The Skandia Folkdance Society is the sponsor each June of *Midsommarfest*, one of the most authentic midsummer celebrations.

Swedish Creative Spirit

**We are not permitted to choose the frame of our destiny.
But what we put into it is ours.**
— Dag Hammarskjöld (1905–1961)
Swedish statesman, Secretary-General of the United Nations

Swedish creativity is the envy of the world. The talents and innovations springing from Swedish inspiration are impressive, especially in light of the size and population of the country that gives birth to these forces. During recent centuries, Swedes have skillfully reshaped impulses borrowed from other cultures, using the elements of its own tradition and historical roots to create something new. Swedish culture is also characterized by a longing for greatness, coupled with the refusal to be pushed into the background. The creations of Swedes often are imbued with a poetic tone that is informed by wit, simplicity, sensitivity, with a love and respect of nature. Swedes bring good taste to the material comforts of life, blending functionalism, crafts-manship, and the innovative use of materials into a unified vision.

These characteristics are clearly seen in today's entrepreneurial Swedish climate. Swedes are great exporters of contemporary music, second only to the United Kingdom and the U.S. Swedish commercial ventures, epitomized by IKEA, Volvo, Saab, Orrefors, Absolut, and H&M (Hennes & Mauritz) department stores, speak to the success of a creative and global approach to business. Swedish cinema with its directors and actors exerts a powerful and influential force around the world.

It is altogether fitting that Sweden is the home of the Nobel Prizes, which annually recognize productive excellence wherever it is found at work in the world. When the leading lights in science, literature, and diplomacy come to Stockholm each year, these Nobel Prize recipients are warmly welcomed to a country powered by a creative spirit.

The Intimate World of Carl Larsson

Carl Larsson, watercolor, Gunlög utan mamma (Gunlög without Mama), *1913, The American Swedish Institute, Minneapolis, Minnesota*

The watercolors of Carl Larsson (1853–1919) are especially appealing in the series showing his home in the village of Sundborn in the district of Dalarna. Larsson and his artistic wife Karin took possession of the house in the late 1880s; by 1901 the household included seven children.

The more children, the more prayers

I guess I should start telling you about all these simple pictures from my home, with all those children. It all started very quietly and simply...there were those rainy weeks in Sundborn when Karin encouraged me to realize an old idea, to draw all the walls of the little cottage as a family keepsake....I put in one child here and another one there just to get some life into the pictures....This was all going on...parallel with my other artistic activities....and perhaps that is the reason why it became the most immediate and lasting part of my life's work. For these pictures are of course a very genuine expression of my personality, of my deepest feelings, of all my limitless love for my wife and children.

— Carl Larsson

From Larsson's autobiography, first published as *Jag* ("I"), 1931; translation *Carl Larsson, The Autobiography of Sweden's Most Beloved Artist,* published by Penfield Press, 1992.

Anders Zorn

*There have always been two
etchers, Rembrandt and myself.*
— Anders Zorn, (1860–1920)

A great portrait painter of his era,
Zorn was a contemporary and
friend of Carl Larsson. Zorn also
painted a lively portrait of Bruno
Liljefors. Zorn's graphic work is
also highly regarded.

Right: *Anders Zorn, etching,*
Queen Sophia of Sweden, *1909*
The American Swedish Institute,
Minneapolis

Bruno Liljefors

Bruno Liljefors, oil on canvas, Two Foxes in Snow, *1920*
The American Swedish Institute, Minneapolis

I paint animal portraits.
— Bruno Liljefors, (1860–1939)

John Fabian Carlson

John F. Carlson, oil on board, Across the Pond, *circa 1925*

Study directly from nature...
She will remain forever the foundation of inspiration material.
— John F. Carlson, *Elementary Principles of Landscape Painting*, 1928

Born in Sweden, John F. Carlson (1875–1945) immigrated with his family to Buffalo when he was twelve. Earning a scholarship to the Art Students League in New York, and after working in Colorado, he founded the John F. Carlson School of Landscape Painting in Woodstock, New York. Nationally recognized as a leading landscape painter, Carlson is famous for his lyrical snow scenes. His classic volume, "Elementary Principles of Landscape Painting" has been reprinted three times under the title *Carlson's Guide to Landscape Painting.* This indispensable work has been called "a Bible for beginning painters and serious professionals," and has been in print for over seventy-five years.

Sven Birger Sandzén

*I feel that one should be guided in both composition
and use of color by the character of the landscape.*

— Birger Sandzén

Sandzén (1871–1954) completed his artistic training in his native Sweden, studying with Anders Zorn. In 1894, Sandzén immigrated to Lindsborg, Kansas, taking a position at Bethany College, where he taught for over fifty-two years. A mentor and inspiration to generations of art students, Sandzén became famous for his bold landscapes of the Rocky Mountains in both oil and lithography. His work was recognized by the Swedish Government, which awarded him the Order of Vasa and the Order of the North Star.

Birger Sandzén, oil on canvas, Smoky River, *1921
Birger Sandzén Memorial Art Gallery, Lindsborg, Kansas*

Top: *Oil on canvas,* The Old Homestead, *1921, Birger Sandzén Memorial Art Gallery* **Below:** *Linoleum block print,* Brook with Cottonwood Trees, *1934, private collection*

Carl Milles

Carl Milles, bronze, Sunglitter
A mermaid riding a dolphin, circa 1918
Gustavus Adolphus College, St. Peter, Minnesota
Gift in honor of Donald Gregory and his contribution to the arts at Gustavus Adolphus College
by Paul T. Granlund and Edna Spaeth Granlund, 1982

When you see something beautiful, look a long, long time.

— Carl Milles

Sweden's most famous sculptor, Carl Milles (1875–1955) was christened Carl Emil Wilhelm Andersson. "Milles" was adopted by his father from an army nickname. Born near Uppsala, Milles worked briefly in Rodin's studio. From 1931–1951, Milles was at the Cranbrook Academy of Art in Bloomfield Hills, Michigan, where he was resident sculptor and director of the sculpture department. Cranbrook today possesses one of the world's best collections of sculpture by Milles, on display both outdoors and in the Cranbrook Museum. Examples of his work are seen all around the world, notably his *Monument for Peace* at the Ramsey County Courthouse in St. Paul, Minnesota. The sculpture pictured above, showing a sea nymph astride a dolphin, was once considered too lewd for public view by a Detroit city councilman. Milles' nude sculptures were sometimes controversial, and he had a fig-leaf installer on call. Although he became an American citizen, Milles returned for his last years to an island near Stockholm called Lidingö. Today his home there, Millesgården, has an outdoor sculpture garden displaying his work.

Paul Granlund

South Wind II

Bronze, 1982, Gustavus Adolphus College,
in memory of Rud Lawson

Paul Granlund (1925–2003) was born to a Swedish-American family, and grew up in Minneapolis. His creative career spanned fifty years and over 650 sculptures, which have been described as "deeply spiritual and passionate — a celebration of life, death, birth, resurrection..." More than thirty of his bronze works, including the examples shown here, are on the campus at Gustavus Adolphus College, St. Peter, Minnesota, where Granlund was from 1971–1996 a sculptor in residence.

Photo, Jeanne L. Wright

Dancing Francis

Bronze, 1989, Gustavus Adolphus College,
St. Peter, Minnesota, given by the Anderson
family in memory of Ren and Sylvia
Anderson

I did have to figure out why Francis was dancing. He was dancing for his love of God, his marveling at the universe God made. — Paul Granlund

Photo, Anders Björling

Christ Chapel, Gustavus Adolphus College
St. Peter, Minnesota

© Photo, Joe Lencioni

North Door, Christ Chapel

Paul Granlund, bronze, circa 1961
This entrance depicts seven major points in the second article of the
Apostles' Creed. Other doors at the chapel are titled Hope, Old Testament
and New Testament.

Left: *Christ Chapel, Gustavus Adolphus College, 1961*
Designed by the architectural firm of Setter, Leach & Lindstrom,
Minneapolis, Christ Chapel is located at the center of the campus,
symbolizing the central place of religion at this faith-based college in
St. Peter, Minnesota. The spire rises 187 feet into the air.

The American Swedish Institute

Turnblad Castle, Minneapolis

Swan Turnblad's 1908 mansion contains towers, turrets, mahogany, and elaborately carved woodwork. Some of the art is intrinsic to the house: a two-story fireplace, impressive stained glass window, opulent furnishings, and eleven Swedish tile fireplace stoves are featured in the fascinating interior spaces. A center for Swedish-American art, other collections include textiles, furniture, decorative arts, and modern Swedish glass.

Opposite page, lower left: *American Swedish Institute tile stove (kakelugn) from Sweden is in the reading room. With radiant heat, it is a heat efficient combination fireplace and heating stove.*

The Visby Window, a masterpiece of stained glass, is on the staircase of The American Swedish Institute. A copy of a painting by Swedish artist Carl Gustaf Hellqvist, Valdemar Atterdag Levying Contributions on Visby, *this work is a narrative of the historic episode that took place in 1361 in the Swedish town of Visby on the island of Gotland. The Danish King Atterdag threatened to destroy Visby unless its citizens filled three huge barrels with treasure. This image depicts the reluctance of the Swedes to comply with this demand, and also shows the details of medieval costume, weaponry, and architecture.*

Photos, ASI except Visby Window Photo desk, Rik Sferra

Erickson Interiors, handcarved rolltop desk, 1938

Honoring Alfred Nobel in America

The Nobel Prize Banquet Setting

Alfred Nobel Hall of Science, Gustavus Adolphus College
Site of the annual Nobel conference

The Nobel Foundation granted special permission for The American Swedish Institute to display the table setting shown here. The pieces are for the Nobel Prize banquet held annually in the Stockholm City Hall. The Nobel dinner service includes china by the Rörstrand Porcelain Company, and table linens by Klässbol Linneväveri. A relief portrait of the Nobel medal appears on the linen napkins. Glassware made by Orrefors and cutlery by Gense were both designed by Gunnar Cyrén.

Augustana College, Rock Island, Illinois

Old Main

Photo, Augustana College

The college was founded by Swedish graduates of the universities of Uppsala and Lund. The architecture is in the tradition of Swedish universities.

Olof Krans, Folk Artist of Bishop Hill, Illinois

A Religious Communal Society

Krans came to Bishop Hill from Sweden with his parents in 1850. In 1896, recovering from a fall, he painted over ninety paintings depicting the life and people of the Bishop Hill Colony. At the time of the Colony's fiftieth anniversary, Krans donated many of his paintings to the settlement; today they are preserved in the Bishop Hill Museum which is administered by the Illinois State Preservation Agency.

Olof Krans (1836–1916), oil on canvas, Self Portrait, *1908*

Olof Krans, oil on canvas, Sowing in the Field, *circa 1896*

The Steeple Building, built in 1854, was used for living quarters and a school. The building later became a central Colony administration center. The tower's one-handed clock displays the hour only. The building is shown at right and also below in the photo taken circa 1890. Bishop Hill is open year-round for visitors and has many Swedish festivals and special programs which celebrate heritage.

Photos and illustrations, Bishop Hill Heritage Association

Below: *Midsummer group celebrates with music.*

Swedish Presence in America

Nearly 400 Years of History and Friendship

Photo, courtesy House of Sweden

This architectural rendering shows The House of Sweden in Washington D.C., which was completed in 2006. The building contains a secretariat, sixteen apartments, and an event center. The stunning modernistic building was designed by the Swedish architectural firm Wingårdh Arkitektkontor. It is as much a center for the promotion of Swedish commerce as it is home of Sweden's diplomatic community in Washington.

New Sweden 1638–1988

This U.S. airmail stamp issued March 29, 1988, honored the 350th anniversary of the settlement of New Sweden by Swedes and Finns at the site of Wilmington, Delaware.

Significant Swedes

Swedes in both the old country and the new world are accomplished in their fields. Leaders in artistic creativity, Swedes and the Swedish touch can also be seen in history, politics, science, industry, design, sport, and diplomacy — virtually all areas of human endeavor. Selected descriptions below include a few of the most prominent personalities and their contributions.

Swedish Artists: Tradition and Renewal

Visual arts produced by Swedes have long been influenced by tradition. Sensitive to artistic developments from Germany, Italy, and France, Swedes have made European art their own — adding their interest in folk art motifs and traditional handicrafts. Swedish preoccupation with the decorative, illustrative, and the modern inform the arts of the country. Swedish artists of both genders have long been sensitive to trends in contemporary design, with an ability to anticipate and assimilate ideas of modernity. Especially during the last 150 years, Swedish art is marked by an interest in storytelling, from fairy and troll tales to children's stories. The following brief biographical entries describe a selected group of Swedish artists best-known and most influential in North America.

John Bauer (1882–1918), painter and illustrator, was influenced by the work of Carl Larsson. Bauer's fame rests on his illustrations for an annual Swedish Christmas book called *Bland Tomtar och Troll* ("Among Elves and Trolls"). A part of the national romantic symbolist movement, Bauer's visions brought life to Swedish folk tales and influenced modern filmmakers Jim Henson and Frank Oz in their motion picture, *The Dark Crystal*. Bauer and his family died tragically when a ferry boat capsized in 1918.

Elsa Beskow (1874–1953), author and illustrator, was one of the founders of Swedish children's literature. Her innovative illustrations accompanied her skillful children's stories, which were often drawn from her own childhood experience. Her books have become classics and have been translated into many languages; they are perennially popular and are still in print. Her most popular works include "Flowers' Festival" (*Blomsterfesten i täppan*) and "Pelle's New Suit" (*Pelles Nya Kläder*).

Knut Ekwall (1843–1912), painter, printmaker, and book illustrator, is best known for his vivid painting called "The Emigrants," showing the huddled masses onboard a ship bound for the new world. An artist influenced by the style of the Belle Epoque, Ekwall's work can be seen at the Tranås Badhotell in Tranås, Sweden.

Carl Larsson (1853–1919), realist painter and illustrator, has become one of the world's most beloved artists. Larsson considered his public commissions his most important work, but his private vision of family life in fresh and bright watercolor is the most popular and frequently reproduced. His books depicting a charming home life, including *Ett hem* ("A Home") and *Åt solsidan* ("On the Sunny Side"), are available in English in America. (See also page 33.)

Bruno Andreas Liljefors (1860–1939), wildlife painter and caricaturist, was a close contemporary of Anders Zorn, who painted a handsome portrait of him. Born in Uppsala, Liljefors is justly famous for his intense depiction of the struggle for survival in nature. His mastery of animal painting was a skillful blend of realism and impressionism, and his preoccupation with survival of the fittest depicts nature as a metaphor of nationalist struggle. (See also page 34.)

Jenny Nyström (1854–1946), painter and illustrator, has been called "the mother of Swedish Christmas." Nyström's lifelong interest in Christmas themes and her clever depictions of the *tomte* (gnome) characters have earned her a place in the hearts of people worldwide. *Jultomten* (the Christmas elf) had a strong presence in Swedish tradition in the nineteenth century, and Nyström's endless variations on this theme appeared in magazines, weeklies, and periodicals. Inspired by the fairy tale world of John Bauer, Nyström was also influenced by Swedish folklore. Her versatility as an artist, portrait painter, and craftswoman had been overlooked until recently; the Swedish National Museum in Stockholm honored her with a major exhibition in 1996. The city of Nyström's birth, Kalmar, contains the Kalmar County Museum, sole heir of her estate.

Johan Tobias Sergel (1740–1874), sculptor, studied in Rome and became a leading proponent of the neo-classical style. His sculpted subjects were drawn from mythology, but he also was known for his lively caricature drawings, a valuable record of late eighteenth-century life. Sergel created monumental sculpture in honor of Swedish historical figures, Gustavus Adolphus and Gustav III.

Anders Zorn (1860–1920), realist painter and portraitist, was born in Mora as Anders Leonaardsson, only later taking his paternal name. Famous for his penetrating portraits, Zorn painted three American presidents and many other famous contemporaries. His painted depictions of water effects and nudes are also prized. Today the Zorn Museums in Mora, Sweden, preserve the fascinating history of his life. Zorn Manor preserves a way of life from around 1900; the Zorn Museum contains the artist's own work and his interesting collections; the Gammelgård is an open-air museum with a collection of ancient timber buildings moved from the Mora area. (See also page 34.)

Swedish-American Artists: Inspiration and Innovation

Swedes who became American citizens, as well as the descendants of Swedish immigrants, have provided a Swedish flavor to American art. Tradition is now overlayered with innovative thinking, yet a strong connection to figural depiction and illustration endures. Swedish-American artists were also leaders in regionalism, so much a part of American art of the past century. Women artists continue to make important contributions to Swedish-American art. Sculpture remains a leading medium of expression. This selected list includes the best-known Swedish-American artists.

John F. Carlson (1874–1945), painter, was a leader in landscape painting in New York state and Gloucester, Massachusetts. Partly regional and partly traditional, he mastered the changing moods of nature. (See page 35.)

Paul T. Granlund (1925–2003), sculptor, built on a traditional figural style, making his bronze works immediately distinctive. Often spiritual in content, his sculptures appear all across the Midwest at colleges, churches, and in cities. (See also pages 39–41.)

Jene Highstein (1942–), abstract sculptor, began his career in Chicago after studying philosophy. Now internationally recognized and based in New York, Highstein has been credited with creating monumental minimalist works "with a human face." His large-scale public sculpture and site-specific installations provoke associations with nature and culture.

Helen Hokinson (1893–1949), illustrator and cartoonist, was the daughter of a Swedish ironsmith, and a native of Mendota, Illinois. Hokinson's popular cartoons appeared for nearly twenty-five years in *The New Yorker* magazine, until her untimely death in an airplane crash in 1949.

Lisa Jevbratt (1967–   ), digital artist, was born in Sweden and teaches at San Jose State University in California. Trained as a research theorist and working as an Internet artist, Jevbratt explores the implications of emerging technologies.

Carl Milles (1875–1955), sculptor, is considered more Swedish than American by many critics. Milles lived and worked at Cranbrook in Michigan for twenty years, and only returned to Sweden shortly before his death. (See page 38.)

Claes Oldenburg (1929–   ), sculptor, was born in Stockholm and came to America in 1936. Spending his first years in Chicago, Oldenburg moved to New York in 1956. Exposed to pop art influences, he produced a series of giant public works depicting mundane objects, lending a whimsical element to outdoor sculpture. He has often been called "the thinking man's Walt Disney."

Frederick Remahl (1902–1968), WPA painter, was born in Sweden and christened Frederick Anderson. Remahl became a talented colorist and mid-century modernist, most often associated with Chicago.

Birger Sandzén (1871–1954), painter, was born in Sweden and became famous for his expressive canvases of the Rocky Mountains. Sandzén was a leader of regionalist style and approach. (See also pages 36–37.)

Haddon Sundblom (1899–1976), illustrator, was born in Michigan into a Swedish-speaking family. Sundblom became famous for his images of Santa Claus, created for the Coca-Cola Company, creating a key figure in American Christmas imagery. Toward the end of his life, Sundblom created pin-ups, and covers for *Playboy* magazine.

Gustaf Tenggren (1896–1970), illustrator and animation sketch artist, was born in Sweden and succeeded John Bauer as illustrator for a popular Swedish Christmas book. Arriving in the U.S. in 1920, Tenggren's success as an illustrator for fairy tales led him to Walt Disney, where he began work in 1936. He lent a distinctly Scandinavian style to some of the great classics of Disney animation, such as *Snow White* and *Pinocchio*.

Literary Leaders: Swedish and Swedish-American Writers

> *...I find the joy of life in the hard and cruel battle of life*
> *— to learn something is a joy to me.*
>
> — August Strindberg

Five Giants of Swedish Literature

Selma Lagerlöf

Selma Lagerlöf (1858–1940), novelist, in 1909 became the first female writer (and the first Swede) to win the Nobel Prize in literature. Lagerlöf is particularly noted for *Gösta Berling's Saga, Memories of Mårbacka,* (her childhood home), and the fairy tales, *The Wonderful Adventures of Nils* and *The Further Adventures of Nils Holgersson*. These books stress kindness to animals and a reverence for ecology.

Astrid Lindgren (1907–2002), children's book author, wrote the *Pippi Longstocking* (Pippi Långstrump) series, among the most beloved children's books ever written. Her fairy tales and fanciful stories have been translated into 85 languages. Children from all around the world come to Vimmerby, Sweden, to visit Astrid Lindgren's World, a theme park and garden where characters and places from her stories come to life.

Vilhelm Moberg (1898–1973), author and historian, created an emigrant tetralogy, a series of four novels widely read and admired. The first novel in the series, *The Emigrants,* was made into a popular film in 1971. The other novels include *Unto a Good Home, The Settlers,* and *The Last Letter Home* — all depict the life of Swedish immigrants to Minnesota. The sweeping narrative is the story of Karl Oskar, the self-reliant farmer, and his wife, Kristina, who cannot reconcile herself to the new world. Moberg spent several years in Scandia and Lindstrom, Minnesota, researching the details for his epic tale.

Photographed as silhouettes, these bronze statues of Moberg characters show Karl Oskar facing west, and his wife Kristina looking back to Sweden. Situated at the port city of Karlshamn, these sculptures symbolize all emigrants who left their homelands for the new world. Nearby is the old emigrant hotel, now a museum in Sweden. This historic place is on the itinerary of Dean and Charlotte Anderson's Scandinavian tours, originating in Lindsborg, Kansas.

August Strindberg (1849–1912), playwright and writer, is among Sweden's most important writers and was a pioneer of modern European theatre. His often autobiographical novels and plays reveal the hypocrisy of nineteenth-century society, questioning gender roles and morality. Strindberg was a socialist and progressive thinker; his dramas moved from naturalistic to symbolic as he grew older. Among his most famous plays are *Miss Julie* (*Fröken Julie*) and *The Ghost Sonata* (*Spöksonaten*).

Per Anders Fogelström (1917–1998), novelist, was a leading figure of modern Swedish literature. A native of Stockholm, Fogelström wrote a series of novels about the city. Only one is available in English translation, *Stockholm: City of My Dreams* (*Mina Drömmars stad*).

Other important Swedish literary voices include: Per Atterbom (poet/historian), Carl Michael Bellman (poet/composer), Fredrika Bremer (feminist author), Albert Engström (artist/writer), Erik Axel Karfeldt (poet), Pär Lagerkvist (author/poet), Axel Munthe (physician/writer), Georg Stiernhielm (poet/linguist), and Esaias Tegnér (poet/writer).

Famous Swedish-American Literary Voices

Ray Bradbury (1920–), science fiction and mystery writer, was born in Illinois to Swedish immigrant parents. Starting in 1938, Bradbury built his career to its current popularity, with many of his works adapted to radio, television, film, and theatre. His most famous pieces include *The Martian Chronicles* and *Fahrenheit 451*. In 2004, Bradbury received the National Medal of Arts award.

> *My father wrote no letters. He did no writing at all. He had never learned to write. When his father and mother died in Sweden his schooling had only taught him to read...he became a teamster at the distillery, finally laying by enough money to buy steerage passage to America, to "the new country where there was a better chance."*

> — Carl Sandburg, from *Always the Young Strangers*

Carl Sandburg (1878–1967), poet and biographer, was born to a Swedish immigrant family in Galesburg, Illinois. First working as a journalist, Sandburg published his early poems between 1914 and 1918, which catapulted him to international fame. He began his four-volume biography of Lincoln in 1926, and his autobiography, *Always the Young Strangers*, is a classic story of immigrant assimilation. Winner of two Pulitzer Prizes, Sandburg has been called "...an American in every pulse-beat."

Above: *The Carl Sandburg Birthplace, an Illinois Historic Site, Galesburg*
Below: *Carl Sandburg's living room and writing studio, where he spent the final years of his life, at his country home,* Connemara, *now a national park service site, near Flat Rock, North Carolina. His typewriter sits on an orange crate.*

Gustaf Elias Unonius (1810–1902), cleric and writer, led a group of Swedish immigrants to a short-lived settlement in New Uppsala, Wisconsin, in 1841. Although Unonius returned to Sweden in 1858, his impact as a writer from America was impressive; his letters home helped spark a wave of Swedish immigration. Unonius later published his two-volume memoir, *Pioneer in Northwest America, 1841–1858.*

Famous Swedes

H.M. King Carl XVI Gustaf and Queen Silvia of Sweden visiting Gustavus Adolphus College, St. Peter, Minnesota, in 1996.

Carolus Linnaeus (1707–1778), natural scientist, is more often known in Sweden by the name he used after his ennoblement in 1757, Carl von Linné. One of the most famous botanists, physicians, and zoologists in history, Linnaeus is the father of modern ecology as well as the father of modern taxonomy, the system of scientific classification used for flora and fauna. In 1732, Linnaeus was one of the earliest explorers of what was then called Lapland. He has been called the "Prince of Botanists."

Paul Granlund, bronze, Linnaeus, Head of Carl von Linné, *1988.*
Gustavus Adolphus College, St. Peter, Minnesota

Emanuel Swedenborg (1688–1772), scientist, theologian, and mystic, began his career as an inventor anticipating many modern scientific inventions. In 1747, with the onset of spiritual visions, Swedenborg pursued a higher calling, revealing the doctrines of the second coming and writing spiritual interpretations of the *Bible*. His last work, *The True Christian Religion*, opposes the doctrine of the Trinity, emphasizing love as the core of Christianity. Fifteen years after his death, Swedenborgianism as an organized religion began in London. Often called "The New Church," its tenets are based on Swedenborg's writings and were especially popular in the nineteenth century. Organized in America in 1817, "The New Church" influenced Americans as diverse as Johnny Appleseed, Walt Whitman, and Helen Keller. Today, the Swedenborgian Church in North America has approximately 1,500 members.

Alfred Nobel (1833–1896), inventor and philanthropist, began as a youth to study explosives. In 1867, he patented a mixture called "dynamite," followed by patents and inventions of other nitroglycerin combinations. After becoming known as a "merchant of death," Nobel decided to leave his fortune to create annual prizes to be given without distinction of nationality. Every year since 1901, Nobel Prizes in physics, chemistry, physiology or medicine, literature, and peace have been awarded to recognize international achievements. In 1968, the Nobel Foundation added an annual prize in economics. With the exception of the Peace Prize that is presented in Oslo, Norway, the Nobel Prizes are presented by the King of Sweden in Stockholm each December.

Dag Hammarskjöld (1905–1962), economist and diplomat, was the son of a Swedish prime minister. After some experience in business, Hammarskjöld moved into the diplomatic world and was a delegate to the Paris conference that established the Marshall Plan in Europe after World War II. Coming to the United States in 1951, Hammarskjöld served as its second Secretary-General from 1952 until his death in 1961. During a peacekeeping effort in Africa, Hammarskjöld died in a plane crash and posthumously received the Nobel Peace Prize in 1961. His only book, *Markings* (*Vägmärken*), was a spiritual diary, first published in 1963.

Wallenberg is a great example to those of us
who want to live as fellow humans.
— H. M. King Carl XVI Gustaf
dedication of Stockholm's Wallenberg monument, 2001

Photo, The Raoul Wallenberg Committee of the United States

Raoul Wallenberg

Raoul Wallenberg (1912–?), diplomat and humanitarian, was a member of a wealthy and prominent business family. Wallenberg received a degree in architecture from the University of Michigan in 1935. Posted as a Swedish diplomat at Budapest in 1944, Wallenberg used his diplomatic status and Swedish neutrality to save Hungarian Jews from the Holocaust. Skillfully negotiating with Nazi officials, he prevented the final destruction of the Budapest Jewish ghetto. In 1945, Wallenberg was arrested by the Soviets during the liberation of Hungary. Documents later showed that Wallenberg died in Soviet imprisonment in 1947, but this account has been contradicted by numerous Wallenberg sightings, some as late as 1990. In 1981, Wallenberg was made an honorary citizen of the United States. Monuments, memorials, and streets are named for him all over the world. The *Raoul Wallenberginstitutet* was established in 1984 at Lund University in Sweden for research and education regarding international human rights.

Additional Swedes of Note

The number of famous Swedes far exceeds our ability to describe them all. The following list is a reminder of the leading role that Swedes have played on the international stage.

In the world of music, Johanna Maria Lind, "Jenny Lind," (1820–1887); Jussi Björling (1911–1960); Birgit Nilsson (1918–2005); and Astrid Varnay (1918–2006) were among the most famous vocal artists of their time. ABBA is one of the most popular of all modern rock music groups.

Among entrepreneurs, Ivan Krueger, "The Match King," (1880–1932) and Gustaf de Laval (1845–1913), engineer of steam turbines and dairy machinery, are outstanding.

Björn Borg (1956–) in tennis; and Annika Sörenstam (1970–) in golf are two modern wonders of athletic accomplishment.

Scientists of note include Anders Celsius (1701–1744), famous for his invention of the Celsius temperature scale in 1742.

Swedish diplomats must include Axel von Fersen (1755–1810), the statesman who was a great friend of Marie Antoinette; and Folke Bernadotte (1895–1948), famous for his efforts to free concentration camp victims at the end of World War II, who was assassinated while acting as an official U.N. mediator in Palestine.

With the highest visibility of any Swedes in history, filmmakers and cinematic actors from Sweden have had a huge impact on world culture. Ingmar Bergman (1918–) is one of the leading film directors in cinematic history, bringing to life his own scripts and profound visions. One of Ingmar Bergman's often-employed actors, Max von Sydow (1929–) has a high visibility among American audiences; Greta Garbo (1905–1990) was perhaps the most photogenic film actress in history; and Ingrid Bergman (1915–1982) was as beautiful and accomplished as any actress ever to appear on the screen. Representing a new generation of Swedes in cinema is director Lasse Hallström (1946–), who began his career creating music videos for ABBA.

The Swedish-American Touch

Photo, Anders Jahrner, Tre Fotografer, AB

H.M. King Carl XVI Gustaf of Sweden, left, presents the Royal Order of the Polar Star to Bruce Karstadt, President and CEO of The American Swedish Institute, Minneapolis, 2003. The Order of the Polar Star (Nordstjärneorden), first awarded in 1748, is given today to non-Swedes who have made significant contributions in the service of Sweden.

Five Prominent Swedish-American Personalities

John Ericsson (1803–1889), inventor and engineer, was born in Sweden; but immigrated to New York in 1839. As early as 1854, Ericsson made designs for an iron-clad armored battleship. During the American Civil War, Ericsson built the iron-clad *Monitor*, which scored a major victory for the Union, routing the Confederate's iron-clad *Merrimac*. This battle in 1862 spelled the end of wood naval ships worldwide. Despite over fifty years in America, Ericsson was buried in Sweden. Today major monuments to Ericsson stand in New York City's Battery Park and on the mall near the Lincoln Memorial in Washington, D.C.

Mamie Doud Eisenhower (1896–1979), first lady of the U.S., 1953–1961, was the granddaughter of Swedish immigrants on her maternal side. Born in Boone, Iowa, Mamie married Dwight Eisenhower, thirty-fourth president, in 1916. Among the nation's most popular first ladies, Mamie's recipe for "Million Dollar Fudge" was widely reproduced and became a hit across the country. (See page 149.) Various White House staff members claim to have seen Mamie's apparition in the White House kitchen during the years since her death.

Curator Larry Adams stands in front of the birthplace of Mamie Doud Eisenhower, Boone, Iowa. The living room displays a family Bible. The house is open to the public under the supervision of the Mamie Doud Eisenhower Birthplace Foundation.

Roger Tory Peterson (1908–1996), naturalist and ornithologist, whose father emigrated from Sweden, was one of the founders of the twentieth-century environmentalist movement. Peterson first published his famous *Guide to the Birds* in 1934. This popular volume was followed by five further editions and was the first modern field guide. Peterson won the Presidential Medal of Freedom; it has been said of him that "...no one has done more to promote an interest in living creatures...."

William H. Rehnquist (1924–2005), lawyer and jurist, Chief Justice of the Supreme Court, was born in Milwaukee; his grandparents had emigrated from Sweden in 1880. Rehnquist became an Associate Justice of the Supreme Court in 1972, and served as Chief Justice of the Court from 1986 until his death in 2005. He was one of only two Chief Justices of Swedish descent; the earlier Chief Justice Earl Warren had shared Swedish and Norwegian ancestry.

Charles Lindbergh, Jr. (1902–1974), aviator and conservationist, was a descendant of Swedish immigrant grandparents on his paternal side. Lindbergh's grandfather left Sweden in 1859 under a cloud. Found guilty of embezzlement, he fled to America with his mistress and an illegitimate son, Lindbergh's father. His son, Charles Lindbergh, Jr., will forever be remembered as the American hero of aviation for achieving the first non-stop solo flight across the Atlantic in 1927. He and his wife, Anne Morrow Lindbergh, the famous writer, suffered the loss of their first child under mysterious circumstances in 1932. An out-spoken and misguided Lindbergh became an active advocate of isolationism and appeasement before World War II. Lindbergh played an important part in the development of commercial aviation, and wrote *The Spirit of St. Louis*, which won a Pulitzer Prize.

Above: *The Spirit of St. Louis at the National Museum of Air and Space, Smithsonian Institution, Washington D.C., and, at right, Lindbergh portrait* **Left:** *Lindbergh's boyhood home, Little Falls, a Minnesota Historical Society site*

They crossed the Atlantic, everybody knows, long before Columbus; then Lindbergh flew it first; and it's a fair guess, if they ever get to tinkering with the Godard rocket, they'll be the first to reach the moon.
— William Seabrook, 1938

This prophetic statement came true in 1969 when Buzz Aldrin, descendant of Swedish immigrants, became the second human to walk on the moon.

Swedish Folk Arts

Some may argue that food ways are among the most important folk arts brought to America with Swedish immigrants. The more traditional categories of folk handicraft, now universally acknowledged as art, are a rich Swedish heritage. Straw craft, wood and birch crafts, wrought iron, woven baskets, Sami crafts, ceramics, and many types of textile work are a few of the many skilled areas in which Swedish craftsmen and women excel.

Dala painting, most often associated with Swedish heritage, is a revival of a style of wall painting that flourished more than a century ago in the *Dalarna* (Dalecarlia) province in central Sweden. Executed in a distinctive style, the earliest paintings were of buildings, fancifully dressed folk, and floral sprays. Many of these early paintings were solemn and religious. Today's emphasis is on flowers; *kurbit* leaves are a characteristic of *Dalarna* painting. In the *Book of Jonah*, chapter 4, the *kurbit*, meaning plant or gourd, is a symbol of both vitality and death. Bright floral designs are used today to decorate chests, chairs, tabletops, and other painted surfaces.

One of the most active decorative painters in America is Karen Jenson from Milan, Minnesota. Karen was born to Swedish-American parents in Clinton, Minnesota, and came to a love of Swedish dalmålning through an early exposure to Norwegian rosemaling. For over thirty years, Karen has been creating Dala painting and teaching across the country. Serving several times as a master in the folk arts apprenticeship program of the Minnesota State Arts Board, Karen has placed her work in many churches, businesses, and houses in southwest Minnesota and beyond. (To view photographs of her home in Milan, Minnesota, see pages 66-67.)

The Dala horse is Sweden's best-known national symbol. In the early 1840s, the first Dala horses were made as toys from pine and spruce scraps left over from furniture and other woodcrafting. Swedish folk arts are enjoying a revival in the younger generations. In addition to growing interest among amateur enthusiasts, sophisticated artists in both Sweden and America draw inspiration from traditional Swedish folk art for innovations in modern design.

Folk Art and Folk Traditions

Dala Painting Sampler

*Painted by the late Helen Elizabeth Blank, former teacher,
The American Swedish Institute, Minneapolis*

A Visit to Karen Jenson
Noted Folk Artist in Milan, Minnesota

Karen Jenson is an award-winning artist and teacher of Scandinavian folk arts.

Karen's home features her art in every room as well as on the kitchen cupboards shown here.

Above:
*Swedish
bedroom*

Left:
Bedroom door

Right:
*Bedroom
cupboard with
towel holder*

This display of Easter decorations is by the Svea Club at The American Swedish Institute, Minneapolis. The rooster, a main Easter motif in Sweden, is shown with other decorations, including Easter witches and painted eggs in cups. Eggs or crocuses may be displayed in natural grass with tiny chicks. The decorations often include feathered birch branches, German paper eggs, and yellow paper napkins.

Swedish Easter customs are a charming blend of folklore and Christian theology. In olden times, one could be awakened on Easter morning by a spanking of birch branches, to be reminded of the suffering of Christ. On Easter Eve, bonfires were lit to scare off the witches and gunshots (today, firecrackers) were fired to prevent the milk cows from drying up. Marita Håkansson, of Minneapolis writes *"Easter in Sweden is almost as big as Christmas — four days long and a wonderful fiesta of flowers, newly opened birch leaves, and, of course, the food. We usually serve gravlax — cured fresh salmon with mustard and dill sauce — roasted young chickens, new small potatoes, and the freshest greens in the salad. Sometimes the first strawberries come to Sweden from Holland and are served for dessert. Very strong coffee and a marzipan tart decorated with little chickens end the meal. Glad Påsk! Happy Easter!"*

Carol Seefeldt, photographer, captures the history of the Gammelgården Museum in Scandia, Minnesota, through all seasons and at special events, shown here and on the following pages.

Gammelgården (an old small farm) is owned by the Elim Lutheran Church. The parsonage preserved there was built in 1868 and is the oldest one existing in Minnesota. Open May to mid-October, the museum features six buildings and guided tours on weekends. An immigrant *hus* (house) built in 1855 was moved to the grounds in 1984 and restored twelve years later. Events include *Midsommar Dag,* Dala painting competitions, *spelmansstämma* (music festival) a *lutfisk* dinner and Lucia celebration.

Swedish Egg Coffee

1/3 to 2/3 cup ground coffee
1 egg
1 tablespoon water
7 to 8 cups cold water
1/2 cup cold water

Gently beat coffee grounds and egg with 1 tablespoon water. Bring 7 to 8 cups of water to a boil in a porcelain or graniteware coffee pot. Add coffee mixture, bring to a boil, and simmer 7 to 8 minutes. Remove from heat. To settle the grounds, add one-half cup cold water. Serve immediately. May be reheated.

Gammelgården: A Special Place

Gammelgården in winter: the 1868 Elim Prästhus *(parsonage)*

Gammelgården in summer: the 1854 first church for the pioneers in a field of brown-eyed Susan flowers

Left: Spelmansstämma
music festival violinist
Above: *Large cement Dala horses
awaiting display and a later auction*

Gammelgården Welcome Center

The main building of the complex, shown above during Midsommar, *contains classrooms and a museum shop, featuring a beautiful chest painted in Dala style by Karen Jenson, and other items in the collection.*

Midsommar *in Minnesota*

Scenes at The American Swedish Institute

Photo, Jan McElfish

Above: *Queen Jenna Bernhardson, Anders Cotty Lowry, and Taylor Afton Spreeman, royalty from the Minnehaha Park celebration of Swedish Heritage Day* **Above right:** *ASI flag procession* **Lower left:** *Anna Gimpl*
Lower right: *ASI* Spelmanslag *Mary Londborg, Nils Wilberg, of the Skatelövs Spelmanslag, from Sweden, Daniel Dahlin, and Julie Anderson*

Photo, John Johnson

Raising the Maypole at The American Swedish Institute

*The musicians and dancers wear traditional Swedish folk costumes.
Decorating with garlands of green leaves and flowers, they raise the Maypole
(majstång) to mark the beginning of summer.*

Swedish Festivals in Lindsborg, Kansas

Both photos © Jim Richardson, Small World Gallery, Lindsborg, Kansas

Above: Midsommar *in Heritage Park. The 1904 World Fair Swedish Pavilion, given by the King of Sweden to Lindsborg, is in the background.*
Below: *The* Svensk Hyllningsfest *is a tribute to Lindsborg pioneers.*

Hyllningsfest *Parade, near Bethany Lutheran Church, Lindsborg*

Sjölunden: *The Swedish Language Village*

Photos, John Borge

Costumes are fun at Sjölunden, *the Swedish language village near Bemidji, Minnesota.*

Unmarried girls wear wreaths at Midsommar *at* Sjölunden *where campers follow traditions.*

Lucia celebration at Sjölunden

Lucia Festivals and Decorations

Lucia celebration attendants (tärnor) *and star boys* (stjärngossar) *at The American Swedish Institute. They are part of a choir presenting traditional music for the annual Lucia celebration.*

Emily Barnard was the 2005 Lucia at Gustavus Adolphus College.

Paper curls are a southern Swedish traditional decoration. This Christmas table setting at The American Swedish Institute depicts the late 1800s. The apple is a magic symbol of love and fertility. In Norse mythology, the goddess Idun is the custodian of the golden apples of youth, eaten by the gods to retain their youth.

The fireplace mantel at The American Swedish Institute is decorated for Christmas with boxwood greens and apples. The original Turnblad mansion brass candelabra are decorated with curled paper.

Set for a formal Christmas dinner at The American Swedish Institute, the table has exquisite settings and Vasa-pattern silverware from Sweden. Two Orrefors crystal vases display red amaryllis; white hyacinths are in an antique hand-painted bowl.

Christmas Morning, Bethany Lutheran Church, Lindsborg, Kansas

Swedish Advent and Christmas

The Advent season is gaining importance in Sweden, with churches crowded on the first Sunday in December. Advent candles and calendars are used in homes, and large paper stars glow from windows.

Early missionaries introduced the Lucia legend into Sweden. The festival honors the first Lucia, of Syracuse in Sicily, martyred for her Christian beliefs around A.D. 300. In today's observance each December 13th, the role of Lucia is taken by the eldest daughter of the household. Dressed in white and crowned with a halo of flaming candles, she dispels the blackness of the season of long nights by carrying saffron buns and steaming coffee to her parents before dawn. A Lucia is selected to represent all Stockholm, and this Lucia and her handmaidens serve coffee to the Nobel prize winners for literature.

The major holiday meal is served Christmas Eve, followed by the joy of Christmas tree and gifts. On Christmas Day, everyone is up early, going to church for the *julotta*, the Christmas service. December 25th is for family, and *Annandag jul*, December 26th, begins the many days of feasting, dancing, and visiting. Anyone wishing to pay respects to the royal family may sign a special book at the royal palace in Stockholm on New Year's Day.

Christmas Memories

by Helen Elizabeth Blanck

Our Christmas was special, as Christmas is to others all over the world. Mother served a spectacular dinner without a lot of fuss. The table was set with a white linen cloth, matching napkins, and lovely bright silver. The china was a wedding gift from my father. The menu was simple by today's standards: relish plate, homemade cardamom bread with butter, either pork roast or turkey, mashed potatoes and gravy, mashed rutabagas, and for dessert, egg coffee and maple mousse served from the large cut-glass bowl. When the last spoon was laid on the dessert plate, Dad cleared his throat and said: "This country has been good to me. I came here from Sweden when I was fourteen years old. I landed in New York City with $4.00. Immediately, I spent twenty-five cents to buy a meat pie from a street vendor. Then I took a train to St. Paul where I was met by my Uncle Andrew. He took me to his home for a reunion with his family, including my brother Carl. How nice it was to see them again and to be accepted into their family. It was wonderful to eat Swedish-style food from their bountiful table. Attending school was no easy matter as I spoke only Swedish. Everything turned out well for me, and I am happy to have a family of my own who are Americans." We children heard this story over and over again, and secretly groaned at the thought of having to hear it another time. But, as the years go by, Christmastime brings back memories of my parents, two gentle people who always did their best.

Swedish Traditions in America

A native of Sweden, Kerstin Olsson Van Gilder kept Swedish traditions meaningful for her husband, John, and their four children in Iowa City, Iowa. On the first Sunday of Advent, the Van Gilders attended church and lighted the first Advent candle. Beginning on Santa Lucia Day, December 13th, Kerstin and the children prepared more than thirty dishes for the Christmas Eve smorgasbord. They even made homemade sausage.

The Christmas tree, cut in the woods, was brought into the house on December 23rd. "We decorated it American-style," Kerstin said. "We didn't use Swedish flags or pretty paper bags that are typical of Sweden." All the other decorations, however, were Swedish. The straw goat next to the Christmas tree was from Sweden. There were other straw decorations, many candles, pig-shaped candle holders, and Swedish tablecloths.

With the Christmas Eve smorgasbord, the Van Gilders enjoyed a traditional tart drink called *Julglögg*. In Sweden, *Julglögg* recipes are kept secret. "There are as many as there are recipes for meatballs in America," said Kerstin. After the smorgasbord, gifts were opened before the dinner of lutfisk and rice porridge.

On Christmas Day, the celebration took an American turn. Stockings were stuffed with practical items. "In Sweden, Christmas parties are given between December 26th and January 13th, St. Knut's Day," said Kerstin. "In the American communities where we've lived, people have often been surprised when we invite them to a Christmas party after Christmas." Now with their children grown and grandchildren present, the Van Gilders continue to have a Swedish Christmas.

Lucia — A Genuine Swedish Folk Tradition

by Charlotte J. Anderson

The custom to celebrate Lucia on December 13th is more popular in Sweden today than ever before. Wherever there are Swedes, or those of Swedish heritage, there is also some kind of Lucia celebration. The origins of this festival may be found in old Swedish folk customs, but it is also an extremely popular living tradition.

For centuries there had been in Sweden a festival in mid-December. A millennium ago, the celebration of Midwinter was just as important to Swedes as Midsummer. In Sweden and many other countries, every day has been given a name, and in older times, days and dates were often referred to by their names.

The name Lucia comes from the Latin, *lux* (light), and December 13th is the Lucia Day, according to the Swedish calendar. The night of Lucia was filled with spooky magic and rules to obey. The darkest night of the year, the trolls and tomtes were out in full force. One of the most important customs was that the threshing must be finished by Lucia night in order for next year's crop to succeed. During the Lucia night, it was also possible to look into your own future.

The old Lucia customs were neither romantic nor had much in common with today's Lucia celebrations. Around the middle of the eighteenth century, new ideas merged with the old ones. The custom of the bride of light in white robe, wings, and with candles spread quickly. No one really knows the origin of the candles worn on the head, but by 1861 Uppsala students celebrated Lucia for the first time. The first public appearance and crowning of Lucia took place in Stockholm in 1927 and was an immediate success. The custom had been observed within the family, club, or organization; from this date on, it turned into a public celebration.

Lucia has held a special place in the hearts of Swedes. Selma Lagerlöf, the Nobel prize winning author, wrote about the Lucia Day legend in her book *Trolls and Humans*. She ends her tale:

> *Never did I see, in those times, a more magnificent sight, than when the door opened up and she entered the darkness of the chamber...Because she is the light, which subdues the darkness, she is the legend, which conquers oblivion, she is the warmth of the heart, that makes frostbitten regions attractive and sunny in the middle of winter.*

Lucia and the Nobel Laureates

by Anders Neumueller
from *Swedish Press*

Every year around Lucia Day, Swedish newspapers describe how the Swedish Lucia once managed to scare a Nobel Laureate in Literature out of his wits. They always speculate on which literary giant it was, and whether the story is at all true.

All Nobel Prize winners stay at Stockholm's Grand Hotel. As the prize ceremonies take place on the anniversary of Nobel's death on December 10th, winners also get to experience the Lucia celebration that takes place each year on December 13th. Many of the laureates have no idea what Lucia is all about, so it is quite a surprise when they are woken up by young voices singing *Santa Lucia* and white-clad maidens serving them coffee and buns. The memory of Lucia with candles in her hair is probably one of the more exotic souvenirs they bring home with them from Sweden.

For one Nobel laureate in 1930, the Lucia experience was less than pleasant. The American author Sinclair Lewis was a heavy drinker, and it is quite likely that he had bouts of delirium. We don't know what went through his mind when he was woken up on a dark morning by a white-clad blonde with candles in her hair. What we do know is that Lewis panicked. He screamed out and hid his head under the blankets. Lucia and her attendants made a quick retreat.

It was really embarrassing, said my mother; she was the Lucia. Fluent in German, English, and French, she was secretary to the head of the Grand Hotel. Also very pretty, she was the natural choice to be the Grand Hotel's Lucia for several years in a row. I still have the autographed volumes presented to her by Pearl S. Buck, Eugene O'Neill, and John Galsworthy; but there is nothing in that collection from Sinclair Lewis!

The Bounty of Sweden

In 1982, Penfield carefully began compiling "Superbly Swedish: Recipes and Traditions." These traditional recipes proved to be very popular with our readers all across the country. Now, almost two decades later, we have included these classic recipes in this new edition with very small changes and notations. In many cases, we have included accompanying information about the contributors and recipe origins from 1983, which is still of interest. For example, there are recipe contributors listed from Upsala College, which closed in 1995; yet we know these tidbits of information are appreciated. We bring these Swedish-American recipes of enduring value — tried and true — to new audiences.

The Swedes, considered to be the richest, strongest, and most worldly of the Scandinavians, are an interesting combination of sophistication and simplicity in their gustatory preferences. They make the most of their country's prime products: pure butter, rich cream, and piquant cheeses; boundless seafood; pork and poultry; root vegetables; and apples, cherries, and berries.

Flaky pastries, creamy puddings, and crisp cookies attest to the high quality of Swedish dairy products.

Eel, herring, cod, salmon, trout, and other fish are the base of many traditional dishes. The cold waters of the Swedish coastline yield halibut, flounder, and cod, as well as shellfish, challenging the creativity of cooks. Herring may be served whole, sliced, cubed, marinated, fried, baked, or jellied and seasoned in myriad ways. The Swedes are adept at baking, frying, grilling, and poaching other fish or disguising them as the fine-ground ingredients of fish balls or puddings.

Swedish cooks have devised many delicious ways to prepare pork, veal, and beef. Lamb has become increasingly popular in recent years. The Swedes lay claim to the invention of the meatball, with literally hundreds of variations. Most combine pork and beef, a thrifty means of extending the expensive beef. Eggs, bread crumbs, mashed potatoes, and a bit of sugar are common ingredients. Some cooks use beer, creating an incredibly light meatball.

Reindeer meat, long the staple of Sami peoples, has become popular. New herds of deer are being raised to fill increasing orders. Chicken and geese are plentiful. Traditional recipes usually call for boiling and roasting, and dried fruits are the favorite fixings.

Swedish salads are made from raw greens, vegetables, and fruits. Also used in the salad bowl are pickled or preserved foods, cooked vegetables mixed with mayonnaise (sprinkled with dill or parsley), cold meats, and fish.

Favorite fresh vegetables are tomatoes, cucumbers, lettuce, peas, carrots, cauliflower, green beans, and red beets. Beets and cucumbers often find their way into pickling jars. The potato, brought to Sweden from the New World in the seventeenth century, is the mainstay of nearly every dinner. Boiled, fried, baked, or grated into delicate pancakes, the potato is welcome, hot or cold. Leftovers are popped into beef and pork dishes. The first new potatoes are eagerly awaited, but the bigger, older varieties also have their uses: in hasselback *(hasselbackspotatis)* style they are peeled and narrowly sliced nearly to the base, basted with melted butter, and roasted until the slices create a fan with crisp edges. French fries are popular with the Swedes, who avoid greasiness by parboiling and roasting the thin strips.

Apples, pears, plums, cherries, and berries grow in Sweden and are eaten fresh, dried, or in preserves or jams. Lingonberries are a great favorite of the Swedes, and cloudberries offer a rare taste experience. Varieties of strawberries and red raspberries abound to fill the jam pots on Swedish tables. Blueberries grow in the wild, and are marvelous in marmalades, preserves, and pastries.

Whatever the Swedes don't grow or catch, they import: artichokes from Spain; oranges from Israel, Spain, Florida, and California; and bananas and pineapple from the tropics, to name a few. With several gourmet monarchs in their past, the Swedes have developed a taste for elegant eating. They also love the plain excellence of the Swedish peasant tradition — the charming cuisine called *husmanskost.*

Swedish Ginger Cookies *(Svenska Pepparkakor)*

The classic thin ginger cookie is a national treat in Sweden. These "pepper cookies" do not contain pepper, but a delicious combination of molasses, cinnamon, cloves, and ginger; they are redolent with spices. In Sweden, the *pepparkakor* are an old tradition, always served with hot coffee, and are an integral part of St. Lucia's Day (13 December), and the *Julbord* at Christmas.

The cookies are shaped, fluted, crisp, and very thin — sometimes only 1/8 thick. They are most often packed in tins to protect their fragile nature and to keep them fresh. In the twentieth century, American tourists brought the tins back from Sweden; nowadays, the tins are widely available with their contents imported from Sweden or Canada or made here in the States. The tins have become collectable and might feature popular reproductions of works by Carl Larsson or Jenny Nyström, or traditional decorative painting. Tins of *pepparkakor* have become bestsellers in America, and the Internet features hundreds of recipe sources for those who prefer to make their own cookies. Recent family traditions include using cookie cutters to make a variety of fanciful shapes. Some families add the tradition of good luck to the consumption of *pepparkakor*. When you make a wish while holding the cookie, press down with one finger. If the cookie breaks into three pieces, your wish will be granted!

Swedish Flatbread or Hardtack *Knäckebröd*

Flatbread, hardtack, and *knäckebröd* are sometimes used interchangeably to describe the hard, flat, unleavened, air-dried crackers of Sweden. What has traditionally identified *knäckebröd* is the use of rye flour and coarse rye meal. This staple has been called "the last of the Viking snacks," "molar-cracking," and "perforated cardboard." It is similar to American rye crisp.

Originating in northern Sweden, this rye crispbread may have been associated with Viking foods. Since rye flour was susceptible to insects, early Swedes would bake enough to last from one milling season to another. The resulting hard cracker would not mold or attract insects. Created in a variety of shapes, this crispbread would be made by Swedish farm wives most often in large, circular, simple rounds with holes in the middle. Large quantities were hung from broomstick handles or poles in the house, and the family could break off pieces and eat them with fresh butter. The dimples in the cracker were made by a special tool with multiple tines formed in a circular pattern.

Today this dry crispbread is perfect with open-faced sandwiches. You may also find varieties with wheat germ, spices, grains, and leavened with yeast or sourdough. This humble cracker is so basic to Swedish life that the popular Swedish contemporary singing sensation named Louise Hoffsten has called her recent album of soulful music *The Knäckebröd Blues*.

Vodka "Burnt Wine"

Long associated with Russia, Poland, and Finland, today's modern vodka products are often linked in America's consciousness with Sweden. Vodka originated in Eastern Europe, and began as a medicine in the context of an herbal alcoholic extract. Rye and wheat are the classic grains for vodka;

Sweden's vodka is wheat-based.

In Sweden, vodka can be traced back to the fifteenth century when distilled spirits called *branvin* (burnt wine) were first recorded. Made from grain or imported wines in the early days, vodka has been a popular national drink in Sweden since the seventeenth century.

Vodka has a long tradition in Sweden. Only since 1979, however, when Absolut Vodka was introduced to America with an amazingly successful ad campaign, has Sweden become the homeland of the world's best-selling premium vodka. Not as popular in Sweden as it is in America, the success of Absolut in the American market is the story of the victory of hype. Sweden's modern success in exporting vodka means entrepreneurial skill should today be included as part of "the bounty of Sweden."

Photo, Vance Dovenbarger

Executive Chef Paul Jacobson offers an entrée in the dining service of Gustavus Adolphus College, St. Peter, Minnesota.

Smorgasbord

Smorgasbord is one of the Swedish words taken directly into the English language. The Swedish *smörgåsbord*, a feast of traditional dishes that Swedes hold dear, is a far cry from the literal translation of its name: "bread and butter table." It is perhaps the best known of Sweden's culinary traditions — and it knows no season.

It's also quite different from the random assortment of foods for which other nations borrow its name. Far from being a spread of leftovers, the smorgasbord is a beautiful collection of delicacies in their prime, meant to be eaten in a special order on a succession of clean plates. (It is often said: "you can pick out a non-Swede when it comes to a smorgasbord by the way he loads everything onto a single plate.")

No smorgasbord can be too big or too varied, but all should contain the classic herring dishes (at least 25 variations are possible), Swedish meatballs, and Jansson's Temptation, the potato casserole with anchovies, onions, and cream.

The prescribed order for enjoying a smorgasbord begins with herring, a piece of hot potato, and a bit of cheese. Then one picks up a fresh plate and goes on to the fish dishes. One of the most spectacular is *gravlax:* fresh salmon, split, and layered with dill, which has been marinated several days under heavy weights. Smoked eel is another choice for this round. Change plates again and attack the cold meats, such as rolled veal breast, veal aspic, cured ham, salads, and egg dishes. Then, if your eyes aren't bigger than your stomach, you'll fill your plate with the hot dishes like Swedish meatballs, Jansson's Temptation, lamb with dill sauce, cabbage rolls, roast meats, and cooked vegetables. You've arrived at the main course. You may have room for the dark, heavy rye breads or the crisp, hard crackers.

What will you drink? *Aquavit* with the herring is preferred by some, and others recommend beer. The salty, smoky, pickled flavors of the food fight against wine, however.

Can you bear to pick up a clean plate for dessert, or did you eat one bite of smoked reindeer too many? Experienced smorgasbord diners often opt for fruit salad, but Swedish apple cake and cheesecake with lingonberries are other possibilities.

Smorgasbords in restaurants or for important celebrations are lavish beyond belief, but a tempting array for home entertaining might include two or three kinds of herring (as long as one type is pickled), cucumber salad, chopped chives, a ring of sour cream topped with chopped egg, parsley, and sliced radishes served icy cold.

The room temperature line-up might include halves of hard-cooked eggs filled with cod roe and caviar, *gravlax* with mustard sauce, liver paste, and assorted cheeses with rye breads and hard crackers.

Desserts might offer a choice between fresh fruit salad and *ostkaka* (cheese cake) with lingonberries.

Hours melt around the smorgasbord table as guests quaff *aquavit* and beer with the many courses and finish the delightful dining experience with a steaming cup of good Swedish coffee. From start to finish, the smorgasbord is a work of art, lovingly created and consumed.

The American Swedish Institute
Typical Smorgasbord Offerings

Herring in sour cream sauce
  Eggs with mayonnaise and shrimp
    Gravlax (marinated salmon) with sweet dill/mustard sauce
      Smoked turkey breast
        Waldorf salad
          Fishgratäng (cod in cream sauce)
            with cheese, mushroom, and shrimp

AND

Herring in wine sauce
  Smoked sausages
    Pickled cucumbers
      Swedish cheeses
        Fresh fruit
          Red cabbage
            Meatballs
              Swedish sausage
                Boiled potatoes

AND!

Jansson's Temptation
(baked dish of potatoes, onion, and anchovies)

AND!!

Ostkaka (Swedish cheesecake) with strawberry jam and whipped cream

Appetizers and Beverages

Jansson's Temptation

by Anders Neumueller, *Swedish Press,* June 2006

You realize that a humble Swedish potato dish has hit the big time when it is the subject of an article in the *Boston Globe*. The newspaper presents three theories on how Jansson's *frestelse* or Jansson's Temptation got its name. I am going to offer a fourth. The first theory is that the anchovy and potato gratin was named after the famous religious zealot and self-appointed prophet, Erik Jansson who in the nineteenth-century led a large group of Swedes from *Biskops kulla* in Uppland to Bishop Hill in Illinois. Pastor Jansson was, according to hearsay, very fond of the dish, rich on anchovy, cream and potato, and aware of its calorie content, called it his "temptation."

Another theory is that the dish became popular in the 1920s and was named after a contemporary movie called *Janssons Frestelse*. The first film with that name was shown on board *M/S Kungsholm's* maiden voyage to New York in 1928. (The second one came in 1936.) A third theory points to the dish being named after the food-loving opera singer Pelle Janzon (1844–1889), but this association was first made in an article in 1940. Now comes my two cents worth. When I was a kid my mother used to call upon a *Fröken* Jansson to prepare the dinner when she was entertaining. Miss Jansson also cooked for my grandfather and other families in Stockholm, and she had to be booked months ahead. She was a true professional who refused to have anything to do with the serving, but she always took care of the dishes before she left. The only criticism I ever heard about her was that she always helped herself quite liberally from the wine that was served. Miss Jansson always claimed that it was she who had invented Jansson's Temptation. This happened one late evening when a desperate hostess had rushed out into the kitchen and told her to serve a "vickning" — a late night supper — and the only ingredients Miss Jansson could find were potatoes, onions, cream and anchovy. She was very specific about the family (although I have forgotten the name) and the party where this happened, in the 40s. I don't believe her claim was ever investigated, but I always promote this theory of the origins of Jansson's *frestelse* in honour of *Fröken* Jansson, who really was a masterful cook.

Jansson's Temptation
Janssons frestelse

Miss Jansson

6 medium potatoes
2 large onions
14-16 Swedish anchovy fillets
(4-1/2 ounces)
1-1/2 cups heavy whipping
cream
salt, white pepper
1 tablespoon dry bread
crumbs
1-2 tablespoons butter

Preheat oven to 425°F (225°C).
Peel onions and chop finely. Peel
potatoes, rinse and cut into thin
strips. Spread onions and anchovy
fillets in a shallow buttered baking
dish. If a stronger taste is preferred,
add 1-2 tablespoons anchovy brine.
Cover with potato strips. Add just
enough cream to cover the potatoes.
Sprinkle with bread crumbs and
dot with butter. Bake for 45-50
minutes.
   — from Anders Neumueller

Editor's Note: Jansson's Temptation
is a very popular Swedish smorgasbord dish, usually served along with
other warm dishes during the second
phase of the meal. Scandinavian
anchovies differ from those usually
found in the U.S. This dish should
be served with Swedish hardtack
and butter.

Jansson's Temptation
Janssons frestelse
*Margareta Mattsson, a PhD lecturer
in literature at Upsala College. She
says, "Contrary to what is written,
ordinary anchovies make very good
Jansson's. Just do not include the oil
they are canned in."*

2 medium Spanish onions,
sliced
3 tablespoons butter or
margarine, divided
4 to 5 medium potatoes
2 (2-ounce) cans anchovy
fillets or Swedish or
Norwegian anchovy
fillets (use a little of the
salty brine if using
Scandinavian anchovies)
1-1/2 cups whipping cream,
divided

Sauté the onions in 1 tablespoon
butter until soft. Peel potatoes and
slice length-wise thinly, as for shoe-
string potatoes. Butter baking dish,
layer potatoes, onions and
anchovies, finishing with a layer of
potatoes. Dot with remaining butter.
Bake at 400°, adding half of the
cream after 10 minutes. After 30
minutes reduce heat to 300° and
bake for another 30 minutes.
Casserole is ready when potatoes
are soft. Serve immediately. Serves
at least 10 as an appetizer. Freezes
well; you may have to add a little
more cream when reheating if dry.

Pickled Herring
Inlagd Sill

Irma Greenspan of The American Swedish Historical Museum in Philadelphia sends her recipe for pickled herring, a popular Swedish appetizer. James Moniz, Montclair, New Jersey, suggests packing the herring in small jars as gifts for friends.

3 salt herring fillets
2 red onions, sliced
1 cup wine vinegar
1 cup sugar
1/2 teaspoon white pepper
2 tablespoons crushed
  allspice
1 bay leaf
5 whole cloves

Skin, bone and rinse herring. Soak in cold water overnight. Drain and cut into 1/2-inch slices. Place in glass container, layering with the onion. Make a brine by bringing remaining ingredients to a boil. Let stand until cool and then pour over herring. Refrigerate for 2-3 days, making sure brine covers herring completely.

Variations: James Moniz uses 1-1/2 tablespoons pickling spice instead of the individual spices. Kerstin Van Gilder of Iowa City uses 1/2 cup sherry for half the vinegar and garnishes the herring with chopped fresh dill. She says: "It's good for breakfast, lunch, or any smorgasbord!"

Hot Anchovy Canapés
Varm Ansjovissmörgås

Margareta Mattsson, Larchmont, New York, inherited this handwritten recipe from her mother. Her friends call this dish "Swedish Pizza."

3 tablespoons butter or
  margarine
7 slices white bread (may use
  very thin white bread)
1 large onion, chopped
1 (2-ounce) can anchovies
  (about 14 fillets)
14 teaspoons catsup
  grated Parmesan cheese

Butter bread slices and halve each diagonally to make 14 pieces. Sprinkle each slice with 1-1/2 teaspoons chopped onion. Top each one with one anchovy fillet. Spread one teaspoon catsup on each fillet, and sprinkle generously with Parmesan cheese. Bake at 375° for 10 minutes or until lightly browned. Can be made ahead and frozen. After thawing, reheat for 5 minutes in 400° oven.

Swedish Proverb

Hunger is the best seasoning.

Marinated Salmon
Marinerad Lax

Gustavus Adolphus College

1 (4-pound) whole salmon
2 to 3 cups salad dressing
2 unpeeled cucumbers,
    thinly sliced
4 lemons, thinly sliced

Poach salmon in water to cover and bring water to 140°. Split in half. Place on tray, cut side down. Chill. Frost entire fish with salad dressing and garnish with alternating rows of cucumber and lemon slices (to resemble scales of fish). Refrigerate overnight to allow flavors to blend. Serves 10.

Fruit Punch Liquor
Glögg

James Moniz: "I am a professor of economics at Upsala College, East Orange, New Jersey. I became 'Swedish' by marriage. This recipe was handed down to me by my father-in-law. He was the glögg-maker of the family." The fruit mixture is very good in Glögg *Cake. (See page 146.)*

4 oranges, seeds removed
2 small lemons, seeds
    removed
1 cup pitted prunes
1 cup raisins
7 to 8 cinnamon sticks
20 cracked cardamom pods
24 whole almonds
20 whole cloves
4 (25-ounce) bottles
    California port wine
25 ounces (1 fifth)
    190-proof grain alcohol
    or **aquavit**

Cut oranges and lemons into eighths. Combine all fruit and spices in a large pan. Cook for 20-30 minutes into a "fruit soup," stirring occasionally. While fruit is cooking, pour wine into a large porcelain pan. Cover and bring to a boil, but do not cook. Pour fruit mixture into wine pan. Cover and bring to a boil again. When mixture begins to boil, pour in the alcohol, cover and bring to a boil again. Turn off heat. Holding the cover of the pan at rim of pan as a shield, ignite the mixture with a match. Let burn for 30 seconds, and replace cover on pan. Strain fruit mixture for other use. Bottle. Tastes best when served warm.

Editor's Note: Glögg, *the common Swedish Christmas punch, means "glow," and the name derives from the burning of the sugar over the drink. Today* glögg *is often served less strong, made exclusively of dry red wine. Ready-mixed* glögg *spices are available in Scandinavian food stores.*

A treasure at The American Swedish Institute, the Simon Gate bowl with engraved crystal, was created by Orrefors of Sweden in the 1920s. The vase depicts figures from classical mythology in a style highlighting engravers' skills.

Christmas *Glögg*
Julglögg

*Swedish Crown restaurant and
The Vasa Club, Lindsborg, Kansas*

- 1 **bottle Swedish aquavit**
- 1 **bottle claret, Burgundy or other dry red wine**
- 10 **cardamom seeds**
- 5 **whole cloves**
- 3 **pieces dried orange peel**
- 4 **dried figs**
- 1 **cup blanched almonds**
- 1 **cup raisins**
- 1 **(1-1/2-inch) cinnamon stick**
- 1/2 **pound sugar cubes**

Pour spirits into kettle. Add remaining ingredients except sugar cubes, cover and heat slowly to boiling point. Remove from heat. Put sugar in sieve with long handle. Dip into hot liquid to moisten. With a match, ignite sugar and allow it to burn. Continue dipping sieve into liquid until sugar has melted into *glögg*. Cover kettle to extinguish flame. Cool. Store in closed bottles. Heat before serving, but do not boil. Serve hot in wine glasses with a few raisins and almonds in each glass.

Soups

Blueberry Soup
Blåbärssoppa

Cecile Swenson, Duluth, Minnesota, says, "This is the traditional drink offered to cross-country ski racers during and after a race." Her grandparents came to the U.S. from Sweden in the mid-1800s. She grew up enjoying traditional Swedish foods and later earned a home economics degree from Gustavus Adolphus College.

  4 cups fresh or frozen
      blueberries
  2 quarts cold water
1/2 cup sugar
  1 slice lemon
  1 cinnamon stick
  4 tablespoons cornstarch
1/4 cup cold water
1/4 cup dry sherry (optional)

Place blueberries, 2 quarts water, sugar, lemon, and cinnamon stick in large saucepan. Simmer over low heat until fruit is soft (about 30 minutes). Mix cornstarch with 1/4 cup cold water, and stir mixture and sherry into berry liquid. Continue stirring over low heat until soup is slightly thickened. Serves 6. This may be made ahead and served hot or cold. Carried in a thermos bottle, it is delicious on a ski trip or a winter picnic.

Fruit Soup
Fruktsoppa

Esther A. Albrecht, Moline, Illinois, is a retired teacher of Scandinavian descent. "While we used fruit soups especially during the summer, it is good any time. Sometimes we had it as a bedtime snack."

1/2 cup dried prunes
1/2 cup dried apricots
1/2 cup seedless raisins
  3 cups cold water
  1 stick cinnamon
  2 large apples, peeled, cored,
      and sliced
  2 pears, peeled, cored, and
      sliced
  1 (8-ounce) package dates,
      chopped
  1 1-pound can unsweetened
      sour red cherries with
      liquid
  1 (3-ounce) package cherry
      gelatin
  1 cup boiling water

Place prunes, apricots, and raisins in large saucepan. Add cold water and soak fruits one hour. Add cinnamon stick, apples, and pears. Simmer over low heat 15 minutes; add dates and cherries with liquid. Bring mixture to a boil. In separate pan, dissolve gelatin in one cup boiling water. Stir into fruit.

Chill overnight. Serve with a bit of sour cream, a lemon slice, and a whole date. Serves 8.

Swedish Fruit Soup
Fruktsoppa

Mrs. Wendell A. Johnson, Ames, Iowa, says, "We serve this fruit soup during the Christmas holiday season — for breakfast Christmas morning and for our 6 a.m. St. Lucia Festival, December 13. This recipe was given to me by my grandmother, who came to America from Skåne, Sweden, in the 1870s."

- 1/2 pound prunes
- 1 cup seeded raisins
- 1 orange, sliced
- 1 lemon, sliced
- 1/4 pound dried apricots
- 4 tablespoons tapioca
- 1 cup sugar
- 1 stick cinnamon
- 3 apples, diced
- 1 (8-ounce) jar maraschino cherries, drained

Soak first eight ingredients overnight in enough water to cover. In the morning add apples and more water and cook until fruit is soft. Add cherries.

May be served hot or cold, as a first course or as dessert. Add whipped cream and slivered blanched almonds for a dessert. Serves 10-12.

Fish Soup
Fisksoppa

Rosemary K. Plapp, Iowa City, has lived in Uppsala, Sweden, and was served this soup by a Swedish friend there.

- 1 leek, thinly sliced
- 2 tablespoons margarine
- 1 teaspoon crushed saffron
- 2 tablespoons flour
- 4 cups fish stock or water
- 1 pound cod fillet, thawed enough to cut into bite-sized cubes
- 5 ounces frozen peas
- 4 ounces frozen cooked shrimp
- 1 (6-ounce) can clams, drained (optional)
- 1 teaspoon salt
- 1/4 teaspoon white pepper
- 1/2 cup fresh dill or 1 tablespoon dried dill
- 1 bay leaf
- 1/2 cup half-and-half

In a large saucepan, sauté leek in margarine until soft, but not browned. Stir in saffron. Add flour and continue to heat. Add fish stock and stir until slightly thickened. Add fish cubes to stock and cook on medium heat for 5 minutes. Add peas, shrimp, clams, and seasonings. Cook until fish and peas are tender (5-10 minutes). Add cream and cook until thoroughly heated. Correct seasonings; remove bay leaf. Serve hot. Serves 6.

This dish can be prepared quickly from ingredients in the freezer. A good bread and green salad would complete the meal.

Diane Heusinkveld

Pea Soup
Ärtsoppa

Cecile Swenson, Duluth, Minnesota, says "for centuries, pea soup and pancakes have been the traditional Thursday night supper in Swedish homes, especially during Lent."

- 2 cups split peas
- 8 cups cold water
  - ham bone, ends of baked ham
- 1 medium onion, chopped
- 1 carrot, grated
- 1 teaspoon salt
- 1/8 teaspoon pepper
- 1 teaspoon ginger (optional)
- 1 teaspoon marjoram (optional)

Rinse peas and discard bad ones. In large saucepan or soup kettle, place peas, water, ham bone and ends,

onion, carrot, and seasonings. Simmer on low heat for 2-3 hours, covered. Stir occasionally. Remove ham bone before serving. Serves 6.

Pea soup can be made ahead and stored in the refrigerator or freezer. Good with croutons sprinkled on top.

Variation: From the Vasa Restaurant, Lindsborg, Kansas: Use yellow Swedish peas and 1 pound lightly salted side pork. It is best to soak the peas overnight in enough water to cover, drain and cook as above.

The American Swedish Institute in Minneapolis features pea soup dinners. The rest of the menu may include special homemade rye bread, cheese, ham, dessert, and coffee.

Photo, Bishop Hill Heritage Association

Copper teapot made in the Bishop Hill Colony, Western Illinois

Salads & Veggies

Herring Salad
Sillsallad

Mrs. Ann R. Engquist, Scandia, Minnesota, translated this recipe from an old Swedish magazine. She is the author of Scandia — Then and Now, *co-author of* The Guide to Swedish Minnesota, *and the curator of the Hay Lake School and J. Erickson Log House Museum at Scandia. She says this colorful, tasty salad can be made ahead of time and is a must at a Swedish smorgasbord.*

> 4 herring, soaked in milk for 8 hours
> 2 cups diced cold boiled potatoes
> 1 cup chopped cooked beets
> 2 Spanish onions, thinly sliced
>
> Dressing:
> 1/2 cup sour cream
> 1/4 teaspoon dry mustard
> 1/2 teaspoon pepper
> 1 teaspoon sugar
> 2 tablespoons vinegar
>
> Garnish:
> 6 hard-cooked eggs, sliced
> sliced beets
> parsley sprigs

Remove skin and bone from the soaked herring and cut into cubes. Add potatoes, beets, and onion and set aside. Make a dressing of the sour cream, mustard, pepper, sugar, and vinegar. Pour over salad and mix. Garnish with sliced hard-cooked eggs, sliced beets, and parsley sprigs just before serving.

Variations: Gunhild Anderson, Minneapolis, suggests serving the salad with whipped cream seasoned with beet juice and garnished with parsley. Kerstin Van Gilder, Iowa City, adds chopped apple.

Cucumber Salad
Inlagd Gurka

Elisabet Heisler is a member of The American Swedish Historical Museum, Philadelphia.

> 1 pound cucumbers
> 1/2 cup Swedish spirit vinegar (or distilled white vinegar)
> 1-1/4 cups water
> 1 cup sugar
> finely chopped parsley

Cut cucumbers into thin crosswise slices. Mix the vinegar, water, and sugar. Set aside for a few minutes, stirring occasionally until the sugar is dissolved. Pour the dressing over the cucumbers and add a generous sprinkling of parsley. Chill for at least two hours before serving.

Egg and Shrimp Salad
Ägg i Majonnäs med Räkor

Greta Hanson Knupke, Gulfport, Florida, was a nurse with Nabisco for many years in Chicago. Her mother, Hulda Hanson, was the author of the family history on the Hanson-Wiberg families.

6 hard-cooked eggs
1 pound shrimp, cooked and cleaned
1/2 cup mayonnaise
1/2 cup heavy cream, whipped
      salt and white pepper to taste
      chopped chives or dill sprigs for garnish (optional)

Halve eggs and place in center of serving plate. Arrange shrimp around the eggs. Mix together mayonnaise, whipped cream, and seasonings. Pour dressing over eggs or serve on the side. May be garnished with chives or dill.

Pea Salad
Legymsallad

Christina Brannstrom is a member of The American Swedish Historical Museum, Philadelphia.

2 cups mixed peas and carrots

3 heaping tablespoons mayonnaise
1 heaping tablespoon sour cream or heavy cream
1 sweet gherkin, chopped

If using canned vegetables, drain until dry. If using fresh or frozen vegetables, cook until tender, drain and cool. Mix mayonnaise and cream together and toss with peas and carrots. Add gherkin. Serves 6.

Mother's Beet Pickles
Mors Inlagda Rödbetor

Carol Roberg Lind, Minneapolis, is a graduate of Gustavus Adolphus College. Her mother created this recipe by remembering how her mother's beets tasted.

1-1/2 pounds beets
1 cup cider vinegar
1/2 cup beet water, reserved from cooking
1 teaspoon celery seed
1 teaspoon mustard seed
1/2 teaspoon pickling spices
1 teaspoon salt
1 cup sugar

Wash beets and scrub well. Cook in water to cover until tender. Drain, reserving 1/2 cup of liquid. Slip off the skins and cut with a ridged vegetable cutter. Bring the vinegar and reserved beet water to a boil. Mix the spices, salt, and sugar. Add to the vinegar mixture and let boil again. Arrange the beets in clean canning jars. Add the hot vinegar mixture to cover beets. Seal, cool, and store in refrigerator. For longer shelf life, boil in hot water bath for 15 minutes. Makes 2 pints.

Creamed Potatoes
Stuvad Potatis

Martha Wiberg Thompson

10 to 12 small new potatoes, boiled
White sauce:
    4 tablespoons butter
    3 tablespoons flour
1-1/2 cups whole milk
      salt and pepper to taste
    1 teaspoon dill weed
      (optional)

Place potatoes in serving dish. Regular potatoes cut in half-inch chunks may be substituted for new potatoes. Mix butter and flour in saucepan over low heat. Slowly add milk until mixture thickens. Simmer several minutes while stirring. Pour white sauce over potatoes.

Red Cabbage
Rödkål

1 tablespoon margarine
1 medium head red cabbage, shredded

1 cup water
1/4 teaspoon salt
1/4 teaspoon cloves
1/4 cup sugar
1/4 cup cider vinegar

Melt margarine in kettle. Put in cabbage and sauté for one minute, stirring. Add water and salt. Cover and cook until tender. Add cloves, sugar, and vinegar. Cook until very tender. Serve hot. Makes 8-10 servings.

Roasted Potatoes
Hasselbackspotatis

Kerstin Van Gilder says, "this is just about the best potato with any roast."

8 medium potatoes
4 tablespoons butter, melted and divided
    salt
3 tablespoons bread crumbs

Preheat oven to 425°. Peel potatoes and slice down through each at 1/8-inch intervals, but do not slice completely through. Pat potatoes dry. Place potatoes, cut side up, in a generously buttered baking dish. Baste potatoes with 2 tablespoons of the melted butter and sprinkle with salt. Bake for 30 minutes. Baste with remaining butter and sprinkle with bread crumbs. Bake another 15 minutes or until done.

Brown Beans
Bruna Bönor

Joanne Kendall, St. Peter, Minnesota, wife of John Kendall, former president of Gustavus Adolphus College, says, "Beginning with my immigrant great-grandparents and John's grandparents, we extend now to the fourth generation living in the United States. My contributions for this cookbook could well be titled 'It's Not Easy Staying Swedish' as each generation's likes and dislikes have brought changes in some recipes from Sweden and the discarding of others."

- 2 cups brown beans
- 1 tablespoon butter
- 1/4 cup brown sugar
- 2 tablespoons vinegar
- salt
- flour, enough to thicken

Wash beans and add to cold water. Bring to a boil and then simmer until tender (about 3 hours), adding more hot water if necessary. When beans are tender, add remaining ingredients. Serve hot.

Variation: Mrs. Leroy M. Johnson, Chicago, adds 3 cinnamon sticks when she cooks her beans and 6 tablespoons dark corn syrup with the brown sugar.

Right: *These horses hang on front porches in Lindsborg, Kansas, where they are made by Hemslöjd.*

Grandma Leadholm's "Beggies"
Rotmos (Swedish Rutabagas)

Martha Wiberg Thompson, Iowa City, says, "People who normally do not like rutabagas like this dish because the potatoes make for a milder taste. My grandmother often made this without the cream cheese, which was not always available, and she used cream instead."

- 1 large rutabaga
- 6 to 8 potatoes
- 1 (3-ounce) package cream cheese or 1/2 cup cream
- salt and pepper to taste

Peel, cut up, and cook rutabaga in small amount of water. Do the same with the potatoes. Mash each of the vegetables and then mix them together. Add the cream cheese or cream and seasonings. Serve hot.

Personalized Dala horse sign

Breads

Flatbread
Knäckebröd

Carol Roberg Lind, Minneapolis, "This is a traditional bread that my mother always made at Christmas until she decided that my recipe was better. It is interesting with any meal."

- 2 cups milk
- 1/4 cup butter
- 1/4 cup honey
- 2 teaspoons salt
- 2 packages dry yeast
- 1/4 cup lukewarm water
- 5 to 6 cups flour
- melted butter
- 2 tablespoons wheat germ

Bring milk to a boil. Add butter, honey, and salt and cool until lukewarm. Soften yeast in the lukewarm water and add to milk mixture. Add about half the flour, mix and beat well. Add enough remaining flour to make a soft dough. Turn out onto a floured board, let rest for 10 minutes, and knead until smooth for about 10 minutes. Place dough in a buttered bowl and butter the surface of dough. Cover and let rise in a warm place until doubled.

Divide the dough into 8-10 pieces. Sprinkle board with wheat germ and a little flour, and roll dough out to about 12x7-inches and 1/8-inch thick. Place on greased cookie sheet and prick thoroughly with a fork. Bake at 375° for 10 minutes. Remove from oven and brush with melted butter. Tear or cut into serving-sized pieces. Freezes well.

Flatbread
Knäckebröd

Mrs. Muriel Engen, St. Louis Park, Minnesota, is an active member of the Idun Guild at The American Swedish Institute in Minneapolis. "This flatbread was served with the first course along with a pineapple boat at the luncheon for the King and Queen of Sweden at the Institute in November, 1982. By special request, the recipe was later given to Countess Wachtmeister, wife of the Swedish Ambassador to the United States."

- 1 cup buttermilk
- 1/2 cup white corn syrup
- 1/4 cup vegetable oil
- 1 cup white flour
- 1 cup cracked wheat flour
- 1 cup whole wheat or graham flour
- 1 teaspoon salt
- 1 tablespoon baking soda

Slightly warm the first 3 ingredients,

and mix well with dry ingredients. Let mixture sit, covered, in refrigerator for several hours or overnight. Roll balls out on pastry cloth or board to the size of a walnut; use generous amount of whole wheat flour to prevent sticking. When rolled out, use a notched rolling pin to make pattern on dough. Bake on electric grill at 350-400°, turning often to prevent burning. Stores well in cool, dry area and can be recrisped in warm oven for a few minutes.

Editor's Note: Beatrice Martinson, St. Peter, Minnesota, who works at the Gustavus Adolphus College bookstore, "The Book Mark," says "flat bread will store for weeks in a tight container, but it never lasts that long because it is simply delicious."

Swedish Hardtack
Knäckebröd

Hulda Edman, Minneapolis, retired public health nurse. "I enjoy making healthful food that pleases the palate as well as the eye."

> 1 **cup milk**
> 1/2 **cup butter or margarine**
> 1/2 **cup sugar plus a pinch**
> 2 **packages yeast**
> 1 **cup warm water**
> 2 **eggs, beaten**
> 1/2 **teaspoon salt**
> 6 to 6-1/2 **cups flour**

Scald the milk. Add butter or margarine and 1/2 cup sugar. Set aside to cool. Dissolve yeast in warm water with pinch of sugar. Let stand for 10 minutes. Add beaten eggs and salt to milk mixture. Then add yeast mixture and flour. Mix, then turn out on board and knead to a soft dough. Place in a warm spot and let rise until doubled in bulk. Punch down and allow dough to rest 10 minutes. Divide into 12-14 equal parts, quickly shaping into round biscuits.

Preheat oven to 400°. Roll out each piece of dough on floured board to thickness of pie crust. Prick with tines of a fork. Place on cookie sheet and bake for 5-6 minutes, until bubbly; turn and bake 5-6 minutes on other side, until flecked with brown. Turn off oven, stack pieces of bread on top of each other on cookie sheet and let stand in oven until oven is cold. This makes the hardtack thoroughly dry and crisp. Repeat the warm oven process the next morning if the crispness does not seem satisfactory.

Hardtack keeps very well because it is dry. Also it freezes well if you can keep it around that long. Hardtack is a superb addition to the smorgasbord table, but any time with any food will do just as well.

Swedish Hardtack
Knäckebröd

Elizabeth (Mrs. Einar) Jaderborg, Lindsborg, Kansas, is a lecturer, historian, and writer who has published Swedish-American history and folklore, sometimes under the pseudonym "Selma Lind." She received this recipe from her mother-in-law, Helen (Ella) Lindstrom Jaderborg, "who was the world's best cook!"

- 1 pint buttermilk
- 1/2 cup sugar
- 1/2 cup butter, melted
- 1 teaspoon salt
- 7/8 teaspoon baking soda
- 2 cups coarse rye flour (or enough to form a thick dough)
- 2 cups white flour

Mix ingredients to make a thick dough and form into balls (1-inch or so in diameter). Roll the balls in additional flour, then roll very thin with a peg rolling pin. An ordinary rolling pin may be used, but the dough must be scored and pricked before baking. Bake on a cookie sheet at 425° until lightly browned. These wafers are delicious with soup, salad, or cheese.

Rusks
Skorpor

Suzanne Soderberg, Iowa City, says when she was growing up, "dunking" rusks at coffee time was a special treat at her grandparents' home in the Swedish colony of Bishop Hill, Illinois.

- 2 cakes yeast or 2 packages dry yeast
- 1/2 cup lukewarm water
- flour
- 1 teaspoon salt
- 1 teaspoon sugar
- 2 cups milk, scalded
- 1 cup shortening
- 2 cups sugar
- 1 cup hot water
- 1 tablespoon salt
- 2 eggs, beaten
- 10 to 12 cups flour
- 3/4 teaspoon ground cardamom seed
- cinnamon, sugar, and cream

Dissolve yeast in lukewarm water; add a little flour, salt and 1 teaspoon sugar to make a thick paste. Set aside and let rise until bubbly. Combine milk and shortening; let cool until lukewarm. Then add 2 cups sugar, hot water, salt, eggs, and yeast mixture. Mix well. Gradually stir in flour to make a stiff dough. Add cardamom. Place in greased bowl and let rise until double. Punch down and knead. Shape into 20 to 24 rolls about 1-1/2x6-1/2-inches. Place rolls in two greased 13x9-inch pans. Let rise again until almost double. Brush with a cinnamon, sugar, and cream mixture. Bake at 350° for 30-35 minutes. These rolls are very good eaten freshly baked, can be frozen, or can be made into rusks.

To make rusks, slice rolls lengthwise about 1/4-inch thick, and place on cookie sheets. Bake at 350° for 15 minutes, turning once halfway through the baking. This recipe makes 8-10 dozen rusks.

Rye Bread
Rågbröd

Jenny Johnson was a former volunteer at The American Swedish Institute in Minneapolis.

- 2 medium potatoes
- 1 quart lukewarm potato water (reserved from boiling potatoes)
- 1 tablespoon salt
- 1/2 cup white sugar
- 2 packages active dry yeast
- 4 cups sifted rye flour
- 1/2 cup sorghum or dark corn syrup
- 2 eggs
- 1-1/4 cups brown sugar
- 1 cup margarine
- 2 tablespoons crushed fennel seeds
- 2 tablespoons crushed anise seeds
- 10 cups white flour, divided

Boil potatoes until soft, mash, and add to potato water. Strain, leaving enough liquid to make one quart potato water. Add salt, white sugar, and yeast to lukewarm potato water and stir. Let stand 10-15 minutes. Add rye flour and beat. Let rise in warm place for 1/2 hour. Mix in sorghum or syrup, eggs, brown sugar, margarine, and crushed seeds, and beat with egg beater.

Add 5 cups of the white flour and continue beating. Turn out on board and knead well for 10 minutes. Let rise in well-greased bowl in warm place until doubled. Form into six small round loaves or six loaves to fit one-pound-sized pans. Bake at 400° for 10 minutes, then at 325° for 40 minutes.

Pearl Sugar
Pärlsocker

Pearl sugar is often used in Swedish recipes for decoration. The grains are larger than granulated sugar and do not melt during the baking process. Pearl sugar is used only for decoration and not as an ingredient in recipes. It can be obtained at food specialty shops.

Swedish Rye Bread
Rågbröd

When Evelyn Young, St. Peter, Minnesota, became Food Service Director at Gustavus Adolphus College, her mother said to her, "Evelyn, you should make Swedish Rye Bread for the students and faculty at the college." This is the special Sponberg *bread recipe that has become a Gustavus tradition. It is reprinted from* All This...and Rye Bread, Too *by Evelyn Young.*

    1   cup milk
    1   cup water
2-1/2   tablespoons shortening
  1/2   cup molasses
  1/2   cup sugar
    1   teaspoon salt
  1/2   teaspoon ground anise
    2   packages active dry yeast
    1   tablespoon sugar
  1/4   cup warm water
    2   cups rye flour
4 to 5 cups white flour

Scald milk; add water, shortening, molasses, sugar, salt, and anise. Dissolve yeast and 1 tablespoon sugar in 1/4 cup water. When milk mixture is lukewarm, add yeast, then rye flour, and mix until smooth. Add white flour until dough is easy to handle. Place in greased bowl and let rise until double. Divide into three balls. Cover and let rest 15 minutes. Form into loaves and place in well-greased tins. Let rise until double. Bake at 375° for 35-40 minutes. After removing from oven, brush with melted butter.

Swedish Pastry
Gifflar

Lilly Setterdahl, researcher at the Swenson Swedish Immigration Research Center, Rock Island, Illinois, has been making gifflar *for years, since she learned to make them in a home economics class in Sweden. She says they are similar to Danish pastry, but fashioned differently.*

      1   egg
      3   tablespoons sugar
    1/4   teaspoon salt
    1/2   teaspoon almond extract
            (optional)
      1   cup warm milk
      1   cake yeast or 1 package
            dry yeast
  2-1/2   cups flour
    1/4   pound soft-spread
            margarine
          flour for rolling out
Glazing:
      1   egg, beaten
     or
      1   cup powdered sugar
      2   tablespoons water
    1/4   teaspoon almond extract

Beat egg with sugar, salt, and almond extract together. Stir yeast into warm milk. Let yeast come to the top of milk, then add egg mixture. Add flour. Mix and beat to a shiny dough. (I usually knead it, too.) Roll dough into a rectangle 1/4-inch thick.

Spread margarine over top. Fold over 1/3 of the long side, then 1/3 of the other long side. Do the same with the short sides. Put this folded pastry in the refrigerator to rest for about 15 minutes. It will rise slightly. Take it out and roll it out as before, spreading with margarine and folding. Let it rest in the refrigerator again and repeat the process one more time. This makes the buns flaky when baked. Finally roll out to 1/3-inch thickness; cut into triangles. Roll the triangles from the long side, tucking the pointed end under. Place on baking sheet and let rise until double. Bake at 375° for about 10 minutes or until light brown. Makes about 15.

For glazing, either brush on the beaten egg before baking *or* brush on the powdered sugar/water/almond extract mixture after baking. If you freeze some of the rolls, put the sugar glazing on just before serving.

These look like dinner rolls, but are lighter and fluffier, and not as sweet as American coffee bread. These are good with strong Swedish coffee.

Swedish Sweet Spice Bread
Kyrddbröd

C. Robert Larson's doctoral dissertation at The University of Iowa was on "The History of the Swedish Solo Song." He and Mrs. Larson live in Waverly, Iowa, where he is on the faculty of Wartburg College. "We are both of Swedish extraction and have many close family ties in Sweden."

- 2 teaspoons fennel seed
- 2 teaspoons anise seed
- 2 teaspoons caraway seed
- 1-1/4 cups water
- 1 cup milk, scalded and slightly cooled
- 1/3 cup molasses
- 1/3 cup white syrup
- 1/2 cup brown sugar
- 2 tablespoons vegetable oil or melted butter
- 2 cups flour (can use rye)
- 1 tablespoon salt
- 2 packages active dry yeast, dissolved in 1/2 cup warm water for 10 minutes
- 6 cups white flour, divided

Add fennel, anise, and caraway seeds to water and bring to a boil. Simmer 5 minutes. Strain and add 1 cup of the liquid to the milk. To this add the molasses, syrup, brown sugar, and oil or butter. Add the two cups of flour, salt, and the yeast mixture. To this add approximately 6 cups of white flour, using the last cup of flour on board or pastry cloth, and knead in to make a stiff dough. Knead well until all flour is absorbed and dough is a smooth ball. Place in a large, well-greased bowl, and grease the top of the dough. Place in a warm spot to rise until doubled in bulk (up to 3 hours).

Turn out onto breadboard or pastry cloth to rest for 10 minutes. Form dough into loaves: 2 large loaf pans, 3 round loaves, or 5 small loaf pans. Let rise again until doubled. Bake at 350° for 20 to 30 minutes, depending on size of loaves. Place a sheet of foil loosely over the tops of the loaves during the last 10 minutes of baking to avoid overbrowning. Grease loaves with butter when removed from pans.

Freezes well. Excellent with mild cheeses or ham and a zesty beverage.

Christmas Bread
Julbröd

Gustavus Adolphus College Food Service, St. Peter, Minnesota

- 1 package active dry yeast
- 1/4 cup warm water (105-115°)
- 3/4 cup lukewarm milk, scalded then cooled
- 1/4 cup sugar
- 1/4 cup margarine, softened
- 1 egg
- 1/2 teaspoon ground cardamom
- 1/2 teaspoon salt
- 1/2 cup raisins
- 1/2 cup chopped dried mixed fruit
- 1/4 cup slivered almonds
- 3-1/4 to 3-1/2 cups flour, divided
- 1 cup powdered sugar
- 1 to 2 tablespoons milk
  maraschino cherries
  walnuts

In large bowl, dissolve yeast in warm water. Stir in milk, sugar, margarine, egg, cardamom, salt, raisins, mixed fruit, almonds, and 2 cups of flour. Beat until smooth. Stir in enough of remaining flour to make dough easy to handle. Turn dough onto lightly floured surface; knead until smooth and elastic. Place in greased bowl, cover and let rise until double. Punch down dough. Roll into a 15x9-inch rectangle on lightly floured surface. Roll up tightly lengthwise. Pinch edge of dough into roll to seal well. With sealed edge down, shape into a ring in a lightly greased pie pan. Pinch the ends together. Let rise until double. Bake for 25-30 minutes at 350°.

Make glaze by mixing powdered sugar and 1-2 tablespoons milk until smooth. Spread ring with glaze, and garnish with maraschino cherries and nuts.

Dala Bread
Dalmaskaka

Dorothy Jensen, Mora, Minnesota, lives on the farm where she grew up. She lived in a four-generation household with her grandparents and great-grandparents, all immigrants from near Mora, Sweden, in the early 1880s. Dorothy remembers eating Dala bread as a child on the days they were short of bread and could not wait for loaves to rise in time for the meal.

1   package active dry yeast
1/4   cup warm water (110-115°)
1   cup hot potato water (saved from boiling potatoes)
2   tablespoons sugar
1-1/2   teaspoons salt
1   tablespoon lard
2-1/2   to 2-3/4 cups unbleached flour

Dissolve yeast in warm water. Put potato water into large mixing bowl and add sugar, salt, and lard. Stir until lard is melted and mixture is cool enough to add the yeast. Add 1-1/4 cups flour and beat until smooth. Mix one cup of flour (or more as needed) in by hand or with a spoon, until dough does not stick to sides of bowl. Turn out onto a floured board. While dough rests, wash and grease the mixing bowl.

Knead dough ten minutes, adding flour as necessary until dough is smooth and not sticky. Put into greased bowl, cover with a towel and put in warm place to rise until double, about one hour. Fifteen minutes before dough has finished rising, set oven at 425°. Cover a 15x12-inch cookie sheet with aluminum foil and place on bottom oven rack to preheat. Punch dough down and roll into a ball on the floured board. Flatten with hand and punch with knuckles into a circle about 12-inches in diameter. Put on preheated cookie sheet and bake 20-25 minutes until nicely browned. Cut into pieces 1-1/2-inches wide and 3-inches long. Serve hot as a dinner bread or with soup or salad at lunch. Serves 4-6.

Coffee Bread
Vetebröd

Rosemary K. Plapp, Iowa City, shares her versatile recipe for coffee bread. It can be varied to make rolls, buttercakes, saffron buns for Lucia Day, or Fat Tuesday buns to be served during Lent.

Dough:
12   tablespoons butter or margarine
2   cups milk
2   ounces yeast
3/4   cup sugar
1   teaspoon ground cardamom
6   cups flour

Filling:

> 6 tablespoons butter or margarine
>
> 1/2 cup sugar
>
> 1/2 tablespoon cinnamon or 2 ounces ground nuts

Topping:

> 1 egg, beaten
>
> pearl sugar

Melt butter in saucepan. Add milk and remove from heat. Crumble yeast into large mixing bowl; add sugar, cardamom and milk mixture. Stir in the flour a little at a time and work dough until smooth and shiny. Cover and let rise for 10 minutes. Turn onto board and knead well. Divide into parts and shape into rolls or loaves. Let rise on baking sheet until doubled. Brush with beaten egg and sprinkle with pearl sugar. Bake rolls at 425° for 5-10 minutes; bake loaves at 400° for 15-20 minutes. Do not overbrown.

If making loaves, divide dough into four parts and roll each piece to a 14x8-inch rectangle. Spread with filling made by mixing together butter, sugar, and cinnamon or ground nuts. Roll up from long side and place on baking sheet. Clip each loaf at 1-inch intervals with scissors held perpendicular to the top. Pull sections out to the sides, alternately, to expose the pattern of the filling. Bake as directed above.

Variations: to make **rolls** *(bullar)*, divide dough into four parts and roll each piece to a 14x8-inch rectangle, as above. Spread with filling and roll up from long side; slice each loaf into 1-1/2-inch thick rounds. Place rounds, cut side up, on baking sheet. Let rise and bake as directed above.

For **buttercake:** make rolls as for *bullar,* but slice the roll into rounds 1-1/4-inches thick. Place rounds, cut side up, into buttered cake pan, about 3/4-inch apart. Let rise and bake as above.

For **saffron buns:** to the basic dough, add **2 tablespoons additional butter, 1 beaten egg** and **1/2 teaspoon ground saffron** with the milk mixture. Pinch off small pieces of the kneaded dough, roll into 8-inch sticks and curl into an S or other shapes. Place a raisin in each curl. Let rise and brush with beaten egg before baking. Do not use filling or pearl sugar topping.

For **Fat Tuesday buns:** *(Fettisdagsbullar* or *semlor)*

Use half of the basic dough recipe. Pinch off small pieces of the kneaded dough and roll into smooth balls. Let rise and brush with beaten egg, but omit pearl sugar. Bake as above. After baking, let cool, covered with a tea towel. Cut a lid off the top of each bun and hollow out inside. Mix these crumbs with **3 tablespoons sugar, 3/4 cup chopped nuts, and 1-1/2 cups** whipping cream, whipped. Fill the buns with this mixture, replace lids, and dust with powdered sugar. Refrigerate. May be eaten as is or in a bowl of warm milk.

Saint Lucia Buns
Lussekatter

Gustavus Adolphus College Food Service, St. Peter, Minnesota

- 2 packages active dry yeast
- 1/2 cup warm water (105-115°)
- 2/3 cup luke warm milk (scalded, then cooled)
- 1/2 cup sugar
- 1/2 cup margarine, softened
- 2 eggs
- 1/2 teaspoon ground cardamom
- 1 teaspoon salt
- 1/2 teaspoon powdered saffron
- 5 to 5-1/2 cups flour, divided
- 1/2 cup raisins
  margarine, softened
- 1 egg, slightly beaten
- 1 tablespoon water
- 2 tablespoons sugar

Dissolve yeast in warm water. Stir in milk, 1/2 cup sugar, 1/2 cup margarine, 2 eggs, cardamom, salt, saffron, and 3 cups flour.

Beat until smooth. Stir in enough of remaining flour to make dough easy to handle. Turn dough onto lightly floured surface; knead until smooth. Place in greased bowl, cover, and let rise until doubled. Punch down dough; divide into 24 parts. Shape each piece into an S-shaped rope; curve both ends into a coil.

Place a raisin in the center of each coil. Place rolls on greased cookie sheet. Brush tops lightly with margarine; let rise until doubled. Mix 1 egg and 1 tablespoon water; brush buns lightly. Sprinkle with 2 tablespoons sugar. Bake at 350° for 15-20 minutes. Makes 24 buns.

Editor's note: Some Swedish cooks leave out the cardamom when saffron is used.

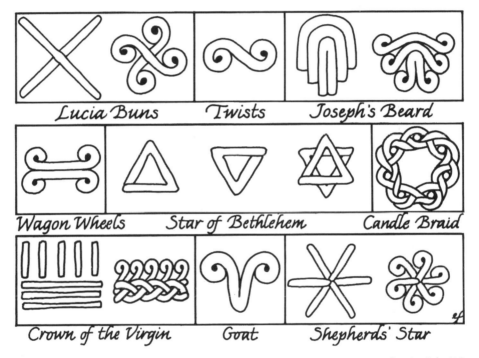

Drawing, Esther Feske

These are the ways to shape saffron dough (or any other yeast dough) for Lucia buns. Raisins accent the curls. Balls of foil hold space for candles during the rising and baking of the candle braid.

Left: *Demitasse cups and saucers from the Swan Turnblad family made by the Rörstrand Porcelain Company, Stockholm; gingersnaps* (pepparkakor), *and Lucia buns* (lussekatter) *for Sankta Lucia Day, The American Swedish Institute, Minneapolis.*

Kringlor
Kringlor

Cecile Swenson, Duluth, Minnesota. This is a rich and fancy bread that seems like dessert and goes well with coffee and tea, breakfast, or fancy luncheons.

Part I:
- 1/2 cup butter
- 1 cup flour
- 1 tablespoon water

Part II:
- 1/2 cup butter
- 1 cup water
- 1 cup flour
- 3 eggs, beaten
- 1 teaspoon almond flavoring

Part III:
- 1 cup powdered sugar
- 1 tablespoon butter, softened
- 1/2 teaspoon almond extract

For Part I, mix together butter, flour, and water. Pat out very thin (1/4-inch) on an ungreased cookie sheet. Set aside.

For Part II, in a saucepan heat butter and water to the boiling point. Remove from heat, and add flour and beaten eggs, stirring well. Add flavoring. Spread mixture on dough on cookie sheet. Bake at 400° for 45 minutes.

For Part III, mix together all ingredients until smooth, and spread on pastry as icing. Serve warm or cold, cut into squares. Makes about 36 squares. Best if served right away, but can be stored, tightly covered, in refrigerator or freezer. If freezing, frost after pastry has thawed.

Almond Paste Twirl
Klippt Längd med Mandelmassa

Gunhild Anderson, Minneapolis

Bread:
3 to 3-1/2 cups flour, divided
- 1 package active dry yeast
- 1 cup milk
- 6 tablespoons butter or margarine
- 1/3 cup sugar
- 1/2 teaspoon salt
- 1 egg

Filling:
- 1/3 cup sugar
- 2 tablespoons butter or margarine
- 1/4 cup ground almonds
- 1/4 teaspoon almond extract
- 1 egg, beaten
- pearl sugar

In large mixing bowl, combine 2 cups flour and yeast. In saucepan, heat milk, 6 tablespoons butter or margarine, 1/3 cup sugar, and salt until just warm (115-120°), stirring constantly until butter almost melts. Add quickly to dry mixture; add egg. Beat at low speed of electric mixer for 1/2 minute, scraping bowl constantly. Beat 3 minutes at high speed. By hand, stir in enough of remaining flour to make soft dough. Knead on lightly floured surface until smooth, 3-5 minutes. Shape into a ball. Place in greased bowl, turning once to grease surface. Cover and let rise in warm place until doubled, about one hour.

Punch dough down and let rest 10 minutes. Roll out to 18x12-inch rectangle. Make almond filling by creaming together 1/3 cup sugar and 2 tablespoons butter or margarine until light and fluffy. Stir in ground almonds and almond extract. Spread almond filling on dough. Roll up from long edge. Pinch to seal edge. Place seam-side down diagonally, or shape into a ring, on a greased cookie sheet. Cut with kitchen shears every 1/2-inch to within 1/2-inch of the bottom. Gently pull slices alternately to the left and to the right. Let rise in warm place until nearly double (about 45 minutes). Brush bread with beaten egg and sprinkle with pearl sugar. Bake in 375° oven for 20-25 minutes.

A powdered sugar frosting is a pleasant alternative to the pearl sugar.

Fruit Twists
Wienersnurror

Midge Frick of Hastings, Minnesota

Rolls:

1-1/2	packages active dry yeast
1	cup lukewarm water
3	eggs
1/2	cup sugar
1/2	cup melted butter
1	teaspoon salt
1	teaspoon ground or crushed fresh cardamom
4-1/2	cups flour
	additional melted butter
1	cup finely chopped candied fruit

Dissolve yeast in lukewarm water. Beat eggs until light. Add sugar, butter, salt, cardamom, and dissolved yeast. Mix well. Stir in flour. Let rise in warm place until doubled (about 2 hours). Punch down and turn out on lightly floured board. Divide dough into 2 parts and roll with rolling pin into 2 rectangles. Brush each rectangle with melted butter and sprinkle with candied fruit. Fold over and cut into 1-inch wide pieces of dough. Twist each piece and place on greased cookie sheet. Let rise again. Bake at 350° for 10-12 minutes. Spread with frosting when cool. Makes about 3-1/2 dozen.

Frosting:
 1 **cup powdered sugar**
 1 **tablespoon butter**
 1 **teaspoon almond extract**
    evaporated milk

Mix powered sugar, butter, almond extract, and enough evaporated milk to be spreadable.

Swedish Pancakes
Pannkakor

Iduna B. Field, Decorah, Iowa, shares this recipe, which her mother brought from Sweden. Her mother made these pancakes to feed her family of nine for breakfast. She did not have a spatula, but flipped the pancakes superbly with a silver knife, and used two round iron griddles at the same time, according to Iduna. Mrs. Field's first name comes from the goddess of Norse mythology, Iduna or Idun, who was the keeper of the apples of youth. When the goddess gave an apple to a mortal, he or she became immortal.

 3 **eggs**
 2-1/4 **cups sweet milk**
 2 **cups flour**
 1/2 **teaspoon salt**
 2 **teaspoons sugar**

Beat eggs until light and mix with milk. Stir in flour, salt, and sugar and beat until smooth. Brush very hot round pancake iron with grease and pour about 1/3 cup batter for each pancake. Spread quickly over full surface of griddle to edges. Turn deftly with spatula. Takes skill, since both batter and pancakes are very thin.

Variation: Mrs. Sigurd L. Anderson, Moline, Illinois, serves large pancakes with lingonberry sauce or blueberry sauce or rolled up and dusted with powdered sugar.

Sourdough Pancakes and Bread
Surdegspannkakor och Bröd

Jon Nelson of Seattle is campus pastor for the Campus Christian Ministry at the University of Washington. "Juni and I have 13 children — three born to us, seven by adoption, and three 'permanent' foster children." The Nelsons are active in the international peace movement. His mother, Ruth Youngdahl Nelson, is a former U.S. Mother of the Year and author of God's Joy in My Heart.

The earliest known forerunner strain of this starter came by covered wagon with the Ziebell family into the Willamette Valley in Oregon. "When you wish to begin a dough for bread or pancakes, take the small jar of starter and add most of it to an equal mixture of flour and warm milk. (Powdered milk mixed with warm water seems to work well.) Let stand overnight or 12 hours, preferably at 80°, the ideal rising temperature. Before adding other ingredients to your dough batter, remove some 'starter' to replenish your original supply. Keep your jar of starter refrigerated between uses, and not too full or too tightly sealed since the cover may pop open. Protect it from other cultures getting in. I keep separate jars of white flour starter and whole wheat flour starter."

Pancakes:

- 2 cups milk
- 2 cups white flour
- 1 sourdough starter
- 3 eggs
- 2 tablespoons sugar
- 2 teaspoons baking powder
- 1 teaspoon baking soda
- 2 tablespoons oil
- 1/2 teaspoon salt

Stir together milk and flour; add sourdough starter. Let stand for 12 hours. Take out enough starter for your next use. Add remaining ingredients, mixing well. Drop batter by 1/4-cupfuls onto hot, greased skillet or pancake griddle. Flip pancakes when tops are bubbly; fry briefly on other side and serve.

Sourdough Bread:

- 2-1/2 cups milk
- 2-1/2 cups white or whole wheat flour
- sourdough starter
- 6 tablespoons sugar
- 1-1/2 teaspoons salt
- 1/2 teaspoon baking soda
- 1 teaspoon baking powder
- 4 tablespoons melted shortening or oil
- 1/3 cup soaked cracked wheat (optional)
- 3 to 4 cups white flour for handling

Stir together milk and flour; add sourdough starter and let stand for 12 hours. Take out enough starter for your next use. Add remaining ingredients, mixing well. Using white flour for easy handling, knead dough and shape into large ball in greased bowl. Let rise until doubled in size. Punch down and shape into two loaves. Let rise in loaf pans. Bake at 350° for 35 minutes.

Editor's note: Sourdough is not Swedish; it is American and western, but thousands of Swedes on the West Coast are confirmed users of sourdough.

Swedish Proverb

The stony earth grows the corn, but the woman does the work.

Swedish Waffles

1-1/3 cups whipping cream,
    whipped
   1 cup flour
  1/3 cup ice cold water (or snow)
   2 tablespoons butter, melted

Fold whipped cream into the flour. Add other ingredients. Let set for an hour. Bake in a waffle iron until brown. This is a crisp waffle. Cool and serve with powdered sugar or lingonberries.

Note: Sour cream can be substituted for a third of the amount of whipping cream.

Swedish Oven Pancake

   1 cup milk
  2/3 cup flour
   2 tablespoons sugar
  1/2 teaspoon salt
   2 eggs
  1/2 teaspoon ground cardamom
  1/4 cup butter

Beat all ingredients except butter until smooth. Place butter in a 9-inch pan and put into a 400° oven until the butter melts. Pour batter into the pan with butter and bake for 35 minutes or until deep brown and puffy. Serves 2.

Swedish Pancakes

Glen and Virginia Arnold, The Swedish Mill, Kingsburg, California

   2 egg yolks
   4 eggs
2-1/4 cups milk
  1/4 cup sugar
1-1/2 cups flour
  1/2 cup butter, melted

Mix all ingredients together. Set aside for at least half an hour or up to overnight in the refrigerator. On a hot griddle spread about 1/4 cup of batter out thinly. Fry on both sides until golden brown. Repeat with remaining batter. Serve with lingonberries, jam, or syrup. Serves 3.

Design by Karen Jenson

Festive Menus

A Feast for Mårtendagen
(November 10)

Kerstin Olsson Van Gilder says, "The Swedes love to celebrate. There is not a single holiday to which we do not add a second day and special foods. The celebration November 10 comes when we are getting used to dark weather. Black soup and sausage are served first, followed by the goose."

Raisin Sausage
Russinkorv

Serve with the Svartsoppa, first course in the Feast for Martin's Day.

   1/2 **cup rice**
1-1/2 **cups milk**
     1 **goose liver**
     3 **ounces calves liver**
     2 **teaspoons flour**
     2 **teaspoons salt**
     1 **teaspoon sugar**
     1 **teaspoon sage**
     1 **egg**
     1 **teaspoon onion, minced fine**
     2 **tablespoons raisins**
     1 **skin of goose neck**

Boil the rice in 1/4 cup water. Add the milk and thicken. Cool the rice. Grind the livers. Mix liver, flour, salt, sugar, sage, egg, raisins, and onions; add to the rice. Fry one small patty for tasting. Add more salt if needed. Stuff loosely in the skin of a goose neck. Sew the ends. Put the stuffed sausage in cold water and heat to boiling. Simmer 35 minutes. Cool. Cut into 1/2-inch slices and serve as a side dish with the soup.

Stock for Black Soup
Svartsoppa

"Veal bones give this soup a mild taste."

1-1/4 **gallons water**
     3 **pounds veal bones**
        goose giblets, wings, and heart
     1 **large carrot**
     1 **medium onion**
     2 **bay leaves**
     2 **teaspoons dried thyme**
     1 **stick whole cinnamon**
     1 **teaspoon whole black pepper**
   1/2 **teaspoon whole cloves**
     3 **apples**

In a stock pot, mix all ingredients together. When the stock comes to a boil, skim off the fat. Let simmer 8 to 10 hours. Strain through a fine sieve or cheesecloth-lined colander. Discard bones and vegetables. This stock may be frozen or used now to make *svartsoppa*.

Black Soup
Svartsoppa

"There is enough to serve 10 to 12 people if you are from southern Sweden (Skåne) and enough for an army if you are from any other part of Sweden.

"When preparing the soup, check for taste. Add more of any of the ingredients as needed. Your taste buds get numb after two or three tastings from the spices, the wine, and the cognac. It is wonderful."

  4 quarts soup stock
  1 quart mixed goose and
      hog blood
  1 cup flour
  2 tablespoons sugar
  1 tablespoon vinegar
  2 tablespoons syrup
1/2 cup red wine
1/2 cup sherry
1/4 cup cognac
  1 teaspoon each salt, pepper,
      ginger, cinnamon
36 prunes
  3 apples

Bring soup stock to a boil. Turn down heat. Add mixture of blood and flour slowly, stirring constantly. Let soup come to a near boil. Take off heat and add rest of ingredients. Strain through sieve. Make the soup one day prior to serving to allow spices to accent the soup.

When heating the soup for serving, stir constantly; do not boil. Serve the soup with boiled or stewed prunes and boiled apple slices added to the soup. There should be three prunes per serving.

Roast Goose
Stekt Gås

This is the second course in the Feast for Martin's Day.

  1 (10- to 12-pound) goose
1/2 lemon
  1 teaspoon salt
1/4 teaspoon black pepper
  8 apples, cored and
      quartered
30 pitted prunes

Wash and dry the goose. Remove fatty portion inside the cavity. Rub the cavity with lemon, salt, and pepper. Fill the cavity with apples and prunes. Close the goose with skewers. Bake in a shallow roasting pan on a rack for 4-1/2 hours at 325°. Check that the juices are yellow and not pink when you pierce it.

Serve the goose with potatoes with parsley. Use the apples and prunes as decorations as well as for serving with the goose. The apples and prunes absorb the fat from the goose. The goose is served after an earlier course of the black soup and the sausage.

Christmas Eve Menu
Martha Wiberg Thompson

Baked Lutfisk with
Cream Sauce and Drawn Butter
Swedish Meatballs
Boiled Potatoes with Parsley
Swedish Mashed Rutabagas
Green Peas
Fruit Salad
Rice Pudding
Assortment of Christmas Cookies

Swedish Dinner Menu
Kerstin Olsson Van Gilder

Ham Rolls
Jansson's Temptation
Herring Salad
Poached Fillet of Sole in
White Sauce with Shrimp and
Mushrooms
Pork Tenderloin
with Orange Sauce
Roasted Potatoes
Pears with Almond Topping

Kerstin Olsson Van Gilder, Iowa City, grew up in a little town near Lund, Sweden, became a registered nurse, and taught nursing in Sweden. In America, she was married in Old Swedes Church in Philadelphia.

Kerstin fondly remembers the yellow pea soup served Thursday afternoons in Swedish college fraternities and sororities with a liqueur punch, followed by Swedish pancakes with lingonberries.

Photo, Barry Bergquist

Angel Chimes

Swedish Proverb

A short man gets a strawberry from the earth quicker than a tall man a star from the heavens.

Main Dishes

Fillet of Sole
with White Sauce, Shrimp, and Mushrooms
Rödspätta med Sås, Räkor och Svamp

Kerstin Olsson Van Gilder, Iowa City

> water
> white wine
> 1/2 onion, chopped
> 1 bay leaf
> 1 carrot, sliced
> 4 fillets of sole

Sauce:
> 2 tablespoons butter
> 2 tablespoons flour
> 1/2 cup poaching liquid from fillets
> 1/2 cup half-and-half
> 1 small can shrimp
> 1 small can mushrooms
> bread crumbs

Put enough water in saucepan to cover fish. Add some wine for flavor, add onion, bay leaf, and carrot and put pan on medium heat. Add sole and poach. Simmer for 4-5 minutes. Remove sole; keep warm. Reserve poaching liquid.

To make sauce: Melt butter in saucepan. Add flour, poaching liquid, and half-and-half. Stir in shrimp and mushrooms, cook until heated through. Pour white sauce over fillets, sprinkle with bread crumbs and place under broiler for 2-3 minutes. Serves 4.

Swedish Marinated Salmon
Gravlax

Karin Persson is a member of The American Swedish Historical Museum, Philadelphia.

> 1-1/2 pounds salmon, cleaned and cut into 2 fillets
> 3 tablespoons sugar
> 3 tablespoons salt
> 1 tablespoon white peppercorns, crushed
> 3 large bunches fresh dill

Combine sugar, salt, and crushed peppercorns. On a large piece of heavy-duty aluminum foil, place one bunch of dill and place one fillet, skin side down, on top. Sprinkle with half of sugar-seasoning mixture. Add second bunch of dill. Add second fillet, skin side up. Top with remaining seasonings and third bunch of dill. Close foil securely and place on a dish or tray. Pile several weights on foil packet. Refrigerate at least 48 hours, turning packet several times. Be sure to keep weights on packet.

Remove salmon and scrape off seasonings. Slice thinly and serve with Swedish Sauce.

Swedish Sauce for Salmon:
- 3 tablespoons prepared mustard
- 3 tablespoons vinegar
- 2 tablespoons sugar
- 6 to 8 ounces oil
- fresh chopped dill, to taste

Combine all ingredients in a jar; cover. Shake vigorously until well blended. Blender can be used. Serve over marinated salmon.

Grandpa Rick's Mustard Sauce
Morfar Ricks Senapssås

Janis Peterson of Stanton, Iowa, preserved the tradition of her Swedish grandparents. At Christmas time this recipe was her father's specialty. "I'm sure it is the only thing he ever cooked!"

- 2 heaping teaspoons dry mustard
- 1 heaping teaspoon flour
- 1 heaping teaspoon sugar
- 1/2 teaspoon salt
- vinegar as needed

Mix together and add boiling water to make a thick paste. Cover and let cool. Thin to desired consistency with vinegar.

Must be made two weeks before Christmas and *must* be served with lutfisk.

Editor's note: This makes a small amount of mustard sauce, but can easily be doubled, tripled, etc.

Lutfisk
Lutfisk

Jeanne Coppage Honette, Stanton, Iowa, writes: "This recipe is from my mother, Minna Hawkins Coppage, the best Swedish cook in town. We had a big cupboard on the back porch where she kept (unbaked) up to 10 mince pies during Christmas. Even after we had a refrigerator, she stuck to the back porch cupboard for her pies, Potatis Korv, Lutfisk, *and Swedish sausages.*

- 1 whole lutfisk

Thick Cream Sauce:
- 3 tablespoons butter
- 3 tablespoons flour
- 1-1/2 cups milk
- 1 cup cream
- 2 tablespoons butter

Drop lutfisk into salted water and cook 7 to 10 minutes. Drain, skin, and remove all bones. Cut up and set in top of double boiler. Make a thick cream sauce and pour over the fish, not stirring much. Add the 2 tablespoons butter and simmer about a half hour. Serve with mustard sauce.

Smoked Salmon with Creamed Spinach and Poached Egg
Rökt Lax med Spenatstuvning och Förlorade Ägg

Countess Ulla Wachtmeister, Swedish Embassy, Washington, D.C., is famed for her excellent cuisine. Her menus are often simple but elegant, and remain true to her Swedish origin. She is also a noted painter.

1 pint heavy cream
2 (10-ounce) bags fresh spinach
2 tablespoons butter
   salt, pepper, and nutmeg to taste
10 eggs
1 tablespoon white vinegar, approximately
10 slices smoked salmon
10 sprigs dill

Simmer cream to reduce by half. Wash spinach and steam in the water that clings to the leaves, 5-7 minutes. Drain thoroughly, pressing to remove moisture. Purée. Return to heat, adding butter and seasonings to taste. Stir in cream. Set aside. Butter pan so eggs will not stick. Poach eggs in water to cover, with vinegar added. Plunge eggs in cold water to stop cooking. Trim off uneven edges. Set aside. Reheat spinach. On ten plates, arrange spinach with a slice of salmon, an egg, and a sprig of dill.

Smelts with Deep-fried Parsley
Stekt Sill med Flottyrkokt Persilja

Countess Ulla Wachtmeister, Washington, D.C.

10 smelts, whole, butterflied with center bone removed
1 to 1-1/2 cups light cream
3 tablespoons Worcestershire sauce
10 teaspoons dill, chopped rye flour
5 tablespoons salted butter
10 large sprigs parsley vegetable oil for deep frying
10 lemon wedges

Marinate smelts for several hours in refrigerator in a mixture of the cream and Worcestershire sauce. When ready to cook, place one teaspoon chopped dill in center of each fillet, close up and dip in flour. Sauté in butter until brown. Remove stems from parsley. Deep fry in hot oil for 5 seconds, then drain. Serve each smelt with deep-fried parsley and lemon wedge. Yields 10 servings.

Smelts may be cooked ahead and reheated for five minutes at 450° or served cold with oil and vinegar dressing.

Editor's note: Barbro Eriksson Roehrdanz of The American Swedish Institute in Minneapolis uses smelts for Swedish recipes that call for *strömming*. This is a small fresh herring unavailable in the United States.

Lutfisk Pudding
Lutfiskpudding

Esther A. Albrecht, Moline, Illinois, is the daughter of the fourth president of Augustana College, Dr. G.A. Andreen.

   3 pounds lutfisk
2-1/2 cups cooked rice
 1/4 pound butter, melted
1-1/4 cups cream
   5 egg yolks, beaten
   5 egg whites, beaten stiff
      salt and pepper to taste
      bread crumbs

Cook the fish. Flake when cool. Add cooked rice, melted butter, cream, and egg yolks. Fold in the egg whites. Season with salt and pepper to taste. Pour into butter casserole and bake at 350° for 35 minutes. Do not fill casserole to top as pudding puffs up when baked. Sprinkle with bread crumbs for last 10 minutes of baking.

Swedish Mantel Clock

Designed by Ken Swisher, and decorated by Shirley Malm, folk artist at Hemslöjd, Lindsborg, Kansas

Photo, Ann Marie Olson

Sailor's Beef Casserole
Sjömansbiff

The Swedish Crown Restaurant, Lindsborg, Kansas

1-1/2 pounds chuck or round of beef
   6 medium raw potatoes
   3 tablespoons butter
   2 large onions, sliced
1-1/2 teaspoons salt
      pepper
1-1/2 cups hot water
 1/2 cup beer
 1/4 cup chopped parsley

Cut meat into 1/4-inch slices and pound. Peel potatoes and cut into thick slices. Heat butter; sauté onion and brown meat. Layer potatoes, meat, and onion in casserole. Sprinkle salt and pepper between layers. End with potatoes. Pour water into frying pan, stir and add liquid to casserole. Add beer. Cover and bake at 375° for 1 to 1-1/2 hours or until meat is tender. Sprinkle with chopped parsley. Makes 4 servings. Good served with pickled beets.

Hash
Pytt-i-Panna

Jean Johnson, St. Peter, Minnesota, and her husband, David, are both graduates of Gustavus Adolphus College. She received this recipe from her mother-in-law, who spent several years of her childhood in Sweden. Hash is a popular and typical Swedish food, about which Jean says, "It is a humble food, undoubtedly peasant in origin, but delicious, economical, easy to prepare and very good for family meals."

4	slices of bacon
1	cup chopped onion
4	cups finely diced boiled potatoes
	butter for frying
2	cups finely diced leftover roast beef
	salt and pepper to taste
	parsley and tomato wedges, for garnish

Cut up bacon and fry. When crisp, remove from pan and sauté onions. Remove from pan. Add potatoes and butter to pan and fry until browned. Add bacon, onion, meat, and seasonings to taste, stirring and frying until heated through. Garnish with parsley and tomato wedges.

Hamburger à la Lindstrom
Biff à la Lindström

Fran von Groschwitz, New York City, makes this favorite late-night snack. She is a direct descendant of Lars Bengtsson, who emigrated to the New World in 1656 on the Swedish ship, Mercurius. *He was one of the early settlers of the Delaware colony.*

1	pound lean ground beef
2	egg yolks
1/2	cup liquid from pickled beets
1/3	cup whipping cream
2	teaspoons salt
	pepper to taste
4	tablespoons finely chopped onion, sautéed in butter (or to taste)
2 to 4	tablespoons drained and finely chopped capers
1/2	cup drained, finely chopped pickled beets
	butter for frying

In a large bowl, mix well the ground beef, egg yolks, juice from pickled beets, whipping cream, salt, and pepper. Gently stir in sautéed onions, capers, and pickled beets. Shape into patties about 2-1/2 to 3-inches in diameter. Melt butter in large heavy skillet over moderate heat and fry patties 3-4 minutes on a side. They should be rosy inside.

Variations: Swedes often serve these hamburgers with a fried egg on top of each patty. Or you can cut small rounds of toast and spread a thick layer of meat mixture completely covering toast. Fry, meat side down, for 2-3 minutes. Place on buttered ovenproof plate, toast side down. Bake at 400° for 5-6 minutes and serve immediately.

Jellied Meat
Sylta

Mrs. Wesley (Eileen) Scott, Minneapolis, says she always knew the Christmas season had begun when she came home from country school and found the pig had been butchered and her mother was preparing to make sausage, head-cheese, and sylta.

- 1 veal shank, cut
- 2 pounds lean pork butt
- 1 tablespoon salt
- 1 tablespoon whole allspice
- 4 bay leaves
      crushed allspice

Place all ingredients in a pot with enough water to just cover meat. Let boil slowly until about 1-inch of liquid remains in pot. Remove meat and set aside to cool. Remove liquid from heat. Cut meat into bite-sized pieces. Put half of meat in a pan. Sprinkle with 1/2 teaspoon crushed allspice. Top with remainder of meat and more crushed allspice. Bring liquid to a boil and strain onto meat. Press meat down with large stone or other heavy object. Chill well and slice to serve.

Meatballs
Köttbullar

Mrs. Wendell A. Johnson, Ames, Iowa, is a graduate of Gustavus Adolphus College. "These meatballs were served in my home every Christmas Eve for the children and any others who did not like lutfisk."

- 1 tablespoon chopped onion
- 1/3 cup bread crumbs
- 2/3 cup water, milk, or cream
- 3/4 pound ground beef
- 1/4 pound ground pork
- 1/8 teaspoon allspice
- 1/8 teaspoon ginger
- 1/8 teaspoon nutmeg
- 1-1/2 teaspoons salt
- 1/4 teaspoon white pepper
- 1/2 teaspoon sugar

Sauté onion in butter. Soak bread crumbs in water, milk or cream. Add remaining ingredients. Shape into small balls. Fry in hot butter. Serves 4 as a main dish. May be frozen in a casserole dish and baked, unthawed, at 350° for 1 hour. Add water or gravy to casserole before freezing.

The Story of Dip in the Kettle
Dopp i Grytan

Gertrude Lundholm, Rock Island, explains that this recipe is traditionally served in Sweden for the noon meal preceding Christmas Eve. This meal helps the busy mother who spends the day preparing for Christmas Eve dinner or Christmas Day smorgasbord. This meal was not served at the table; the entire household, which may have included servants and hired farmhands, helped themselves to a soup bowl, a spoon, and a piece of bread.

At the kettle each person dipped the bread in and with a ladle also took some broth, a chunk of meat, and some vegetables. The beauty of this meal is its simplicity and the communion and fellowship it promotes.

Gertrude and her family like the meal so much that they serve it to friends, using soup tureens at each end of the table. They may add cookies and *glögg* for dessert. They always serve it for Christmas Eve supper. Before partaking of this common meal, young and old alike join hands and dance through all the rooms on the ground floor of the house singing, *"Nu är det Jul igen."*

The Lundholm family recently made this meal for 100 guests of Holden Village, Washington (a retreat center). Before serving it they explained the ritual and the entire community joined hands and danced through the dining hall. Many asked for the recipe and continue the celebration in their own homes.

Gertrude Lundholm says, "Dip in the Kettle is just a hearty soup, and there should be lots of it to satisfy everyone."

Her husband was a professor of music at Augustana College for 47 years. The Lundholms have participated in many Scandinavian celebrations on campus there. Their daughter is married, lives in Sweden, and carries the native recipes to and fro. Gertrude comes from Swedish grandparents and grew up in Stanton, Iowa, a Swedish community where many homes have Dala horses indicating family names. Each year Stanton celebrates St. Lucia Day, electing a queen and teaching children Swedish dances.

Lori Requist, now from Des Moines, Iowa, was chosen as Santa Lucia Queen in 1978 when she was a senior in Stanton High. Her grandmother, Florence, organized the festival in 1952. Lori says, "Years ago this dish was kept on the back of the woodburning stove and when anyone was hungry, they helped themselves."

Dip in the Kettle
Dopp i Grytan

Gertrude Lundholm's recipe

- 1 (2-pound) chunk beef
- 1 (2-pound) chunk lean pork
- 1 (2-pound) chunk veal (optional)
  salt and pepper to taste
- 1 bay leaf
- 2 rings potato sausage
- 1 large onion, cut up carrots and potatoes, cut in chunks (amount depends on number to be served)

A day or two before serving, cook beef, pork, and veal in large kettle with water. Add salt, pepper, and bay leaf. Cook until tender. Add potato sausage during last 45 minutes of cooking. Let cool thoroughly and skim off all fat. On the morning of the day of serving, cut meats into serving-sized pieces. Bring stock and meat to a boil, adding onions, carrots, and potatoes, and slowly simmer until serving time. Serve from kettle on the stove with bread, hardtack, cold root beer, and cookies for dessert.

This should serve about 15. For economy, less meat may be used. If more broth is desired, bouillon cubes and hot water could be added.

Mama's Dish (Ham Loaf)
Mammas Rätt

From the Swedish Crown Restaurant, Lindsborg, Kansas, comes "an old tried and true family recipe."

- 1-1/2 pounds ground ham
- 1 pound ground beef
- 1/2 cup chopped onion
- 2 eggs, beaten
- 1/2 (13-ounce) can evaporated milk
- 1 (6-ounce) can tomato sauce cracker crumbs, enough to mold mixture together
- 1 (10-ounce) can cherry pie filling
- 1 teaspoon cinnamon
- 1/2 teaspoon cloves

Mix all but last three ingredients together well. Shape into single large loaf in loaf pan or individual small loaves on baking sheet. Bake at 325° for 1 to 1-1/2 hours. The meat loaf without the sauce freezes well. Before serving, heat cherry pie filling, cinnamon, and cloves, stirring constantly. Pour fruit sauce over meatloaf before serving.

Swedish Proverb

The sweetest wine makes the sharpest vinegar.

Potato Sausage
Potatiskorv

Lorraine Anderson of "Boklada," in Grinnell, Iowa, sometimes calls this "Potato Baloney." "This is a bit of a nuisance, but it's worth the effort. You'll have to go to the butcher shop to buy about 10 feet of bologna casing.

"Also needed is a funnel with an approximately 1/2-inch opening to work the ground mixture into the casing. Some electric mixers now have an attachment for this, but my mother and grandmother used a piece from the horn of a cow for the funnel."

10	foot bologna casing
6	pounds potatoes
1-1/2	pounds ground lean beef
1-1/2	pounds ground lean pork
1	medium onion, chopped or ground fine
3	tablespoons salt
3	tablespoons pepper
1	tablespoon allspice

Soak casings in water at least 1/2 hour before using. Grind raw potatoes and mix well with other ingredients. To find out how well you are doing on the seasoning, fry a little patty and see how it tastes. Put mixture into casings. Cut at 12-to 18-inch intervals and tie ends with string, leaving small leeway. Keep in light brine, put a plate on top to keep bologna covered with brine.

Store in refrigerator or similar cool place. Boil bologna rings approximately 45 minutes to an hour. Cut in sections and serve with vegetable and/or salad.

Pâté à la Erick
Leverpastej

Helga Hammarskjold is a member of The American Swedish Historical Museum, Philadelphia.

Pâté:

1	pound chicken livers
1	pound ground sirloin
1/4	pound lean smoked ham, cut into small pieces
2	small cloves garlic, minced
1	large onion, finely chopped
2	eggs
1/2	cup flour
1/2	cup whipping cream salt, pepper, and oregano to taste
2	tablespoons cognac

Rinse, dry, and grind chicken livers. Mix with ground sirloin and ham. Add garlic and onion. In a separate bowl, mix eggs, flour, and cream and fold into meat mixture. Add seasonings and cognac. Place in greased, oblong form, cover with aluminum foil and bake at 350° for 1-1/2 hours. Allow to cool completely before removing from pan. Serve cold with Cumberland Sauce.

Cumberland Sauce:
- 3 to 4 teaspoons dry mustard
- 1/2 cup red wine
- 1/2 cup port wine
- 2 tablespoons finely chopped orange peel
- 2 tablespoons finely chopped lemon peel
- 4 to 6 teaspoons grape jelly
  ginger, cayenne pepper, and vinegar to taste

Mix dry mustard with red and port wines. Add peels and jelly. Add spices to taste. Heat to dissolve jelly. Cool and serve with cold pâté.

Stuffed Cabbage Rolls
Kåldolmar

Carol Erling of Edina, Minnesota, says, "I am of Swedish descent, married to a man from Sweden, and work at The American Swedish Institute in Minneapolis. This recipe came from my stepmother, who was born in Stockholm."

- 1 large head cabbage
- 1/2 cup rice
- 1/2 cup milk
- 1/2 pound ground beef
- 1/2 pound ground pork
- 1 egg
- 1 teaspoon chopped onion
- 1-1/2 teaspoons salt
- 3/4 teaspoon pepper
- 2 tablespoons butter
- 1 tablespoon dark corn syrup
  brown sugar for sprinkling

Core cabbage and gently separate leaves. Drop a few at a time in boiling salted water and cook about 15 minutes. Drain on paper towel. Cook rice in salted water about 20 minutes. Drain and mix with milk. Combine meat, egg, onion, and seasonings and add to rice mixture. Put 1 or 2 tablespoons stuffing on each leaf. Fold over and fasten with toothpick. Brown rolls in mixture of butter and corn syrup.

Place rolls in heavy baking dish and sprinkle with brown sugar. Rinse pan used in browning with a little water and pour over the rolls. Cover and bake 1 hour at 350°, basting occasionally. Add more water if needed. Remove toothpicks to serve. Serve with boiled potatoes and lingonberries. Makes 25-30 rolls.

Diane Heusinkveld

Moose roam in northern Sweden.

Oven Pork Pancake
Ugnspannkaka med Fläsk

Aina Stadin, Burnsville, Minnesota, is a volunteer at The American Swedish Institute, Minneapolis.

- 4 ounces fresh pork
- 1 tablespoon margarine
- 1 teaspoon salt, divided
- 3 eggs
- 3/4 cup water
- 3/4 cup milk
- 1 teaspoon sugar
- 1/2 cup flour

Cut pork into small pieces and fry in margarine and 1/2 teaspoon salt. Whip eggs slightly. Add water, milk, sugar and 1/2 teaspoon salt. Mix and add the flour. Pour over the pork in frying pan and bake at 375° for 30-35 minutes.

Cabbage Pudding
Kålpudding

Faye M. Molander, Lindsborg, Kansas, says, "My interest in Scandinavian cooking comes from having Danish grandparents and being married to a Lutheran pastor with Swedish parents. My interest in heritage is even greater living in Lindsborg, Kansas, 'Little Sweden U.S.A.' and being secretary to the president of Bethany College. We were served this lovely simple dish of cabbage pudding in Sweden."

- 1/3 cup rice
- 2/3 cup water
- 2 tablespoons margarine
- 1 medium cabbage, coarsely chopped
- 1 pound ground pork
- 1 egg
- 1/2 cup milk
- salt and pepper to taste

Cook the rice in the water until done. Melt margarine in large skillet and slightly stir-fry cabbage. Mix ground pork, cooked rice, egg, and milk together. Put half of cabbage in bottom of a large casserole, and cover with meat mixture, topping with remainder of cabbage. Bake at 350° for one hour covered; uncover and bake at 325° for 1/2 hour. Serves 4-5. Good served with applesauce or a fruit salad.

Ham Rolls
Fyllda Skinkrulader

Kerstin Olsson Van Gilder

- 1 cup cooked green peas
- 1 apple, diced
- 1 teaspoon lemon juice
- 2 hard-cooked eggs, chopped
- 1 (10-ounce) package frozen asparagus spears, cooked and chilled
- 1/2 cup heavy cream, whipped
- 1/2 cup mayonnaise
- 1 tablespoon horseradish
- 8 slices boiled ham

Combine peas, apple, lemon juice, and eggs. Chill. Cook asparagus and chill. Whip cream and add mayonnaise and horseradish. Stir dressing into vegetable mixture. Place equal number of asparagus spears on each slice of ham. Top with pea mixture. Roll ham to form logs. Place ham rolls on lettuce to serve.

Pork Sunday Steak
Söndagsfläskkarré

Karin Nilsson, a teacher specializing in helping children with learning problems, is from Bromma, Sweden.

    2 pounds lean pork
    1 pickled cucumber, Polish
       or Kosher style
    6 prunes
    1 teaspoon salt
    1 teaspoon black pepper
    1 teaspoon paprika
2-1/2 to 3 tablespoons margarine
    1 yellow onion, thinly sliced
    8 sprigs fresh parsley
    1 cup beef bouillon
Gravy:
    1/2 pound fresh mushrooms
         salt and pepper to taste
    1/2 cup red wine
         water
    1/2 cup whipping cream
         soy sauce

With sharp knife, make holes in pork and fill with thin slices of cucumber and prunes. Rub the steak with a mixture of salt, black pepper, and paprika. In an ovenproof casserole dish, melt margarine and brown the pork on top of the stove. Add onion, parsley, and bouillon, and bake in oven, covered, at 400° for 1 hour.

To make gravy: Clean mushrooms and fry briefly in a skillet. Add salt, pepper, wine, water, and cream. Simmer until desired thickness is reached. Add soy sauce for color. Adjust seasonings to taste. Slice steak thinly and serve covered with mushroom sauce. Serves 6.

Good served with potatoes or rice. Can be reheated in gravy.

Ham
Skinka

Ragnhild Holm is a member of The American Swedish Historical Museum, Philadelphia.

    1 (10- to 12)-pound ham
    1 cup salt
    1/4 cup sugar
    1/2 tablespoon saltpeter
Brine:
    To every quart of water, add:
    1/2 cup salt
      1 tablespoon sugar
    1/4 tablespoon saltpeter
To cook:
         water
 1 to 2 bay leaves
     10 white peppercorns
         allspice

Coating:
  1 egg white
  1 tablespoon prepared
     mustard or dry mustard
2 to 3 teaspoons sugar
     bread crumbs

Wipe ham and rub with mixture of
1 cup salt, 1/4 cup sugar, and 1/2
teaspoon saltpeter. Place in a clean
wooden or stone crock and refrigerate 1-3 days, turning occasionally.
Make brine of boiling water, salt,
sugar, and saltpeter. Cool and pour
over ham to cover; weigh down
with plate or other heavy object
and refrigerate for 10 days. Remove
ham, wipe well and place, fat side
up, in boiling water to cover.
Return water to boil, add bay
leaves, peppercorns, and allspice.
Simmer until done, about 3 hours.

When cooked, skin ham and
wipe to remove all loose fat. Return
liquid to cool. Brush with mixture
of beaten egg white, mustard, and
2-3 teaspoons sugar, then sprinkle
with bread crumbs. Bake or broil
until nicely browned. Strain liquid
and season. Ham is ready to serve
and liquid can be heated and served
as "dip in the pot (or kettle)."

Right: *Goose basket from Bishop
Hill, Illinois. The goose was held
in the basket while the feathers
were plucked and later the feathers
were kept in the basket.*

Old-fashioned Spiced Ham
Cajsa Wargs Kryddskinka

Rosemary Plapp, Iowa City

1 (7- to 9-pound) ham, cured
   and lightly smoked
2 teaspoons whole cloves
2 teaspoons whole allspice
2 teaspoons rosemary or basil
3 bay leaves
2 teaspoons marjoram or
   oregano

Preheat oven to 300°. Remove rind
and most of fat. Place ham on a
piece of aluminum foil large
enough to wrap entire ham. Place
spices in a mortar and crush well.
Rub ham on all sides with spices.
Wrap ham in foil and seal tightly.
Insert meat thermometer into the
thickest part. Place in oven and
bake until thermometer reads 170°,
about 5 hours. Serves 12-15.

Photo, Bishop Hill Heritage Association

Pork Tenderloin with Orange Sauce
Fläskkarré med Apelsinsås

Kerstin Olsson Van Gilder, Iowa City

  1 pork tenderloin, cut in
     3/4-inch pieces
     salt and pepper to taste
  2 tablespoons butter
1-1/2 tablespoons flour
3/4 to 1 cup beef stock
1/3 cup orange marmalade
1/4 cup white wine
  1 tablespoon soy sauce

Season meat with salt and pepper. Brown in butter over medium heat for 5-8 minutes.

Set aside. Stir flour into fat remaining in skillet. Pour in beef stock, orange marmalade, and wine. Let simmer for 1 minute. Place the meat in the sauce and simmer for a few minutes longer. Serve hot.

Loin of Pork
Fläskkarré

Janeth Greupner, Minneapolis, received this recipe from her grandmother.

 10 prunes, halved and pitted
1/2 cup warm water
  4 pounds loin of pork
  2 teaspoons salt
  1 teaspoon pepper
1/4 teaspoon ginger

Soak halved prunes in warm water for 1/2 hour. Drain, saving liquid. Insert prune deep into pork loin. Rub meat with salt, pepper, and ginger. Place meat in roasting pan and roast uncovered at 325° for 40-45 minutes per pound. Add prune juice to drippings and cook.

Egg Cake
Äggkaka

Joan Wright, Minneapolis, "This is an ideal dish for breakfast or brunch."

1/4 cup butter or margarine,
     melted
  3 eggs
  2 cups milk
1/4 to 1/2 cup sugar
  1 teaspoon salt
  1 cup flour
     lemon juice
     powdered sugar

Pour melted butter into 13x9-inch baking pan. Mix eggs, milk, sugar, salt, and flour in blender; pour into pan and bake at 450° for 20 minutes. Serve immediately. Pierce each serving several times with a fork and sprinkle with lemon juice and powdered sugar.

Oven Omelet with Mushroom Sauce
Ugnsomelett med Svampstuvning

Dee Salmonson, Mora, Minnesota, says, "I requested this recipe from a Swedish relative who converted measurements for me. It's a popular smorgasbord item in Sweden and very delicious. I am a farm wife, mother of three sons, a grandmother of two grandchildren, and have had a lifetime of cooking and baking."

- 4 eggs, beaten
- 3 cups of milk, divided
  salt and pepper to taste
- 2 tablespoons butter
- 3 tablespoons flour
- 1 (4-ounce can) mushrooms (stems and pieces can be used), drained

Mix eggs, 1-1/2 cups milk, and seasonings and pour into greased 9x9-inch casserole. Bake at 350° for 30 minutes or until light brown. While omelet is baking, in a small saucepan stir together butter, flour, and remaining 1-1/2 cups milk. Add mushrooms. Simmer until smooth and thickened. Pour over omelet after removing from oven and serve immediately. Makes 6 servings.

This omelet complements either a formal meal or a buffet. Its simple preparation is its biggest asset.

Swedish Spring Chicken
Vårkyckling

Kerstin Olsson Van Gilder

- 1 whole spring chicken (2-1/2 to 3-1/2 pounds)
- 1 bunch fresh parsley without stems
- 1/4 pound plus 1 teaspoon butter
- 1 tablespoon sugar
  salt and pepper to taste
- 1 cup chicken bouillon
  flour
  half-and-half

Mix parsley with 1/4 pound softened butter. Reserve 1 tablespoon of this mixture and rub the rest inside the chicken cavity. Rub the reserved parsley, sugar, salt, and pepper on the outside of chicken. Brown the whole chicken in another teaspoon butter over medium heat, taking about 30 minutes and rotating the chicken to brown on all sides. Add the bouillon to browned chicken, cover, and simmer slowly about 45 minutes.

Thicken remaining juices with flour and half-and-half. The cook must determine the quantity of flour and half-and-half, depending on the quantity of juice from the chicken. Season to taste. Serve this gravy with the chicken.

Desserts

Rice Pudding Notes

Rice pudding, a staple of the Swedish diet, can be prepared and served in many different ways. Some consider it a dessert; others serve it as a side dish with the day's main meal.

Martha Wiberg Thompson recalls eating "Poorman's Rice Pudding" without eggs in it. "At times, eggs were a luxury."

Marion Edman, Minneapolis, says, "Our mother always made this pudding for our Christmas Eve family dinner. If any was left, it was carefully saved to be used Christmas morning for coaxing sleepy children out of warm beds for early Christmas services, *Julotta*. It always worked!"

Nancy Bell of the Stratford Historical Society in Iowa reports that the family of Agnes Dahleim Sackrison always serves rice pudding as a Swedish Christmas porridge. The person who finds the almond in his or her serving will marry within the year.

Rice pudding was important to residents of the communal settlement of Bishop Hill, Illinois, according to Myrna Hallman of Iowa City. Her grandmother, Clara Broline Hillbrand, was born there in 1861.

Rice Pudding
Risgrynspudding

Mrs. Wesley (Eileen) Scott, Minneapolis, says, "My grandparents came from Traheryd, Småland, Sweden. Their name was Ekberg, my maiden name, meaning 'Oak Hill.' I grew up on a farm in west central Minnesota and graduated from Gustavus Adolphus College.

"I was the home economist for Mt. Olivet Lutheran Church in Minneapolis, considered the largest Lutheran church in the U.S. with a membership of about 11,000. September is stewardship month at Mt. Olivet and we have a series of 16 dinners serving approximately 8,000 people. This rice pudding is served every night and is a favorite of all."

- 1/2 cup rice, uncooked
- 4 cups whole milk
- 1/2 teaspoon salt
- 2 eggs
- 2/3 cup sugar
- 1/4 teaspoon nutmeg
  vanilla to taste

Cook rice in milk with salt in a double boiler until rice is very tender and has absorbed most of the milk. Mix eggs, sugar, nutmeg, and vanilla. Add a little of the hot mixture to egg mixture (to avoid curdling) and then combine all in double boiler, cooking only until thickened. Sprinkle with cinnamon. Serves 6. This can be chilled, but is really best served warm.

Creamy Rice Pudding
Bakad Risgrynsgröt med Lingon

Kenneth H. Johnson, Director of Food Service, Augustana College, Rock Island, Illinois, says, "Augustana College, proud of its Swedish heritage, features several Swedish smorgasbords throughout the year. This pudding is always served and enjoyed by all."

- 1   quart milk
- 1/2   cup rice
- 1/2   cup sugar
- 1/2   teaspoon salt
- 1   cup half-and-half, divided
- 2-1/4   teaspoons vanilla
  lingonberries

Scald milk. Add rice, sugar, and salt. Cook at a slow boil until rice is tender, stirring constantly. Remove from heat. Add 1/2 cup half-and-half and vanilla, and stir thoroughly. Pour into baking dish and bake at 350° for approximately 1 hour, or until top is slightly brown. Consistency should be creamy. Cool thoroughly. Add remaining half-and-half and mix well before serving. Top with lingonberries. Makes 10 servings.

Rice à la Malta
Ris à la Malta

Linnea B. Foster, Madison, New Jersey, a graduate of Upsala College in East Orange, New Jersey, says, "After taking courses in Swedish at Upsala, my current main interest in things Swedish is tracing my family's roots in the Province of Halland and the Island of Öland."

- 2   cups cold cooked rice
- 1/2   cup sugar
- 1   cup whipping cream, whipped
- 1/2   cup slivered, blanched almonds
- 3/4   teaspoon vanilla

Combine all ingredients, folding together gently. Chill completely. Serves 6-8. May be served with raspberry or strawberry sauce.

Hot Soufflé of Prunes
Katrinplommonsufflé

Countess Ulla Wachtmeister, Swedish Embassy, Washington, D.C.

- 2/3   cup finely chopped cooked prunes
- 6 to 7   tablespoons granulated sugar
- 6   egg whites
  butter for pan
  sugar for pan
  powdered sugar
  sweetened whipped cream

Combine prunes with sugar. Beat egg whites until stiff. Fold in prune mixture. Spoon into buttered and sugared 8- to 10-cup soufflé dish. Set in shallow pan containing 1-2 inches of hot water. Bake at 350° for 40 minutes. Remove from oven and sprinkle top with powdered sugar. Serve with sweetened whipped cream. Makes 10 servings.

Carmel Custard
Brylepudding

Jane S. Brissman, Rock Island, Illinois, is a retired Augustana College physical education teacher with a degree in home economics from Purdue University. "My jobs took me into two Swedish communities and I also married into a Swedish family. This recipe came from the late Mrs. Birger Sandzén of Lindsborg, Kansas, wife of the famous Swedish artist." (Art by Sandzén pages 36-37.)

  1 cup sugar
  2 cups milk
  4 eggs, slightly beaten
  1 tablespoon sugar
  1 teaspoon almond extract

Carmelize sugar by melting slowly in a heavy skillet. Pour into a mold or baking dish, coating bottom and sides of dish. Cool. Scald milk. Pour over eggs and add sugar and almond flavoring. Pour into carmel-coated dish. Set dish in pan of hot water 1/2-inch deep and bake at 325° for about 1 hour or until a cold knife comes out clean. Chill in refrigerator. When ready to serve, unmold onto serving dish. Decorate with blanched almonds. Serves 6-8. Can be made a day ahead. May be served with whipped cream topping.

Cheese Cake
Ostkaka

Garnet Requist, Stanton, Iowa, makes over a hundred of these puddings a year and either sells them or gives them as Christmas gifts. "I begin in October and freeze them."

  2 eggs plus 1 egg yolk
  1 cup sugar
  1 teaspoon salt
  1 cup cream
  2 teaspoons vanilla
1/2 teaspoon almond flavoring
  1 tablet rennet
  2 tablespoons lukewarm water
  1 cup flour
  1 cup milk
  1 gallon lukewarm milk
     (100-105°)

Beat eggs, sugar, salt, cream, and flavorings together. Set aside.

Dissolve rennet in water. Mix flour with 1 cup milk. Let stand

1/2 hour, then slice through mixture carefully with a spatula about an inch apart. Let stand another 1/2 hour. Gradually drain off scant 1/2 gallon of whey. Add egg mixture to the curds and beat. Pour into a casserole or a 13x9-inch pan and bake for at least one hour or until golden brown and raised evenly. Loosen edges with a knife. *Ostkaka* will fall as it cools.

Cheese Cake
Ostkaka

Midge Frick, Hastings, Minnesota, said this is her "easy, American version" of the Swedish ostkaka.

2	cups milk
1-1/2	cups half-and-half, divided
1	cup evaporated milk
4	eggs, beaten until light
1/2	cup sugar
1/2	teaspoon salt
2	cups dry cottage cheese
1	teaspoon vanilla
1/4	teaspoon almond flavoring
	sugar and cinnamon

Mix together the milk, 1 cup half-and-half, and evaporated milk, and scald; add eggs. Blend well. Mix together sugar and salt; add cottage cheese. Gradually stir in milk-egg mixture, vanilla, and almond flavoring. Pour into well-buttered baking dish. Bake at 325° for 1-1/2 hours or until thoroughly set. Drain off whey and add remaining half-and-half. Sprinkle with sugar and cinnamon. Serves 6-8.

May be garnished with lingonberries or strawberries.

Bread Pudding
Brödpudding

Jeanne Coppage Honette, said, "Every cook will cherish this recipe...it is so easy and so good." The pudding could be served with grape sauce (kräm).

4	cups milk
2	cups white bread pieces
2	eggs, slightly beaten
1/2	teaspoon salt
3/4	cup sugar
1/2	teaspoon vanilla
3	tablespoons melted butter

Scald milk and mash bread in it. Add eggs, salt, sugar, and vanilla. Over this pour the melted butter. Bake in a flat pan at 300° for at least 1 hour. Serve plain or with grape *kräm.*

Variation: Gunhild Anderson, Minneapolis, used buttered sliced cardamom coffee bread and applesauce in her recipe for bread pudding.

Grape Sauce
Kräm

Laney Wigate, Iowa City, who grew up in Lindsborg, Kansas, and is married to a Lutheran pastor, recommends this typical Swedish sauce, which is often served over puddings, or by itself with a pitcher of cream.

- 3 tablespoons sugar
- 2 tablespoons cornstarch
- 3 tablespoons water
- 2 cups grape juice

Combine sugar, cornstarch, and water; mix to a smooth paste. Heat grape juice and add slowly to paste, stirring constantly. Cook until clear and thickened. Cool before serving.

Pudding
Pannkaka

Mrs. Conrad A. Peterson, St. Peter, Minnesota, says, "This pudding has about the same ingredients as ostkaka, but you do not remove the whey and it makes a smoother pudding."

- 2 quarts cold sweet milk, divided
- 1 cup flour
- 3 tablespoons sugar
- 2 eggs, beaten
- 1/4 tablet rennet

Warm 1 quart milk and stir flour, sugar, and eggs into the remaining cold milk. Pour warm milk into this mixture so that whole mixture becomes lukewarm, Soften the rennet in lukewarm water. Pour into the milk mixture, stirring slowly until mixture just begins to curdle and coats the spoon. Quickly place in oven and bake at 350° until puffed up and brown on top.

Steamed Pudding
Vattenbakad Mjuk Kaka

L. Elaine Brolander, Rock Island, Illinois, says, "This recipe is a family tradition at Christmas. It was brought to the U.S.A. by my grandmother from Luleå, (Nr), Sweden, in 1883. Her mother prepared this rich, simple dessert, so the recipe is over 100 years old. It has been made each Christmas by my great-grandmother, my grandmother, my mother, myself, and my daughter in our respective homes."

- 2-1/2 cups flour
- 1 teaspoon baking soda
- 1/2 teaspoon salt
- 1/2 teaspoon cinnamon
- 1 cup margarine, cut in pieces
- 1 cup raisins, floured
- 1 cup milk
- 1 cup molasses

Sift together flour, soda, salt, and cinnamon. Add, in order, the margarine, raisins, milk, and molasses. Generously grease and flour a

Bundt pan. Pour in mixture. Cover pan with 2 pieces waxed paper secured with string or rubber bands. Place on rack in large Dutch oven. Fill pan with boiling water at least 1-inch up on mold and cover.

Steam in 400° oven for 1-1/2 hours. When finished, remove waxed paper and let stand in 400° oven for 1 minute to dry top. Unmold and cool on rack. Serve hot with warm lemon sauce. Makes 10-12 servings. Freezes well wrapped in foil. Can be made ahead and refrigerated if it lasts that long.

Lemon Sauce:
- 2 **cups boiling water**
- 6 **tablespoons cornstarch**
- 1 **cup sugar**
  juice of 2 lemons
- 2 **tablespoons margarine**

Combine ingredients and boil until thickened.

Pears with Almond Topping
Päron med Toscasås

Kerstin Olsson Van Gilder

- 8 **fresh pears**
- 1-1/2 **cups water**
- 1-1/2 **cups sugar, divided**
- 4 **tablespoons butter**
- 2 **tablespoons flour**
- 4 **tablespoons milk**
- 2/3 **cup sliced blanched almonds**
- 1/2 **teaspoon vanilla**

Cut pears into halves, pare and core. Simmer for about 6 minutes in water and 1 cup sugar. Place on serving dish. To make almond topping, combine 1/2 cup sugar, butter, flour, milk, almonds, and vanilla in saucepan and cook over low heat, stirring constantly, for 2-3 minutes. Spoon over pears and chill for about 1 hour before serving.

Variation: Apples may be substituted for pears.

Photo, Bishop Hill Heritage Association

Left: Melon basket produced in the Bishop Hill Colony in Illinois Artifacts may be seen at the Colony Church, Bjorklund Hotel, or the Steeple Building.

Cranberry Dessert
Lingonsyit med Grädde

Joan Wright, Minneapolis

- 1 quart or 1 package
  cranberries
- 1-1/2 cups boiling water
- 1-1/2 cups sugar
- 2 cups whipping cream
- 3 tablespoons powdered sugar
- 1 teaspoon vanilla
- 2 cups crushed graham
  crackers, approximately

Boil cranberries in water until soft and mash slightly to pop all skins. Add sugar and bring to a boil. Chill. Whip cream. Add sugar and vanilla.
Use your prettiest glass bowl. Alternate layers of crumbs, cranberries, and whipped cream. End with whipped cream and garnish with a sprinkling of crumbs. This can be made a couple of hours in advance.

Editor's note: If a recipe calls for lingonberries and they are unobtainable, cranberries are a good substitute.

Lemon Fromage
Citronfromage

Birgitta Wilson, member of The American Swedish Historical Museum, Philadelphia

- 2 egg yolks
- 3/4 cup sugar
  juice of half a lemon
  grated rind of half a lemon
- 1 tablespoon unflavored
  gelatin, soaked in 2
  tablespoons cold water
- 1 cup hot water
- 2 egg whites, stiffly beaten
- 1-1/4 cups whipping cream,
  whipped
  whipped cream and grapes
  for garnish

Beat egg yolks and sugar until fluffy. Add lemon juice, rind and gelatin, which has been dissolved in hot water, to egg mixture, stirring constantly until thick. Fold in egg whites and cream and pour into mold rinsed with cold water. Refrigerate 3 hours before unmolding and serving. Garnish with whipped cream and grapes. Serve with fancy cookies.

Left: Dala design by Diane Edwards from Swedish Folkart

Produced by Bergquist Imports

Carl Larsson, Now It's Christmas Again, *triptych on tile, 1907 from an original painting in the museum, Helsingborg, Sweden*

Apple Dessert
Äppeldessert

Joanne Kendall, St. Peter, Minnesota

- 8 slices white bread, crusts removed
- 1 cup milk
- 1/2 cup sugar
- 1/2 teaspoon vanilla
- 1 (8-ounce jar) applesauce
- 1-1/2 to 2 cups whipping cream, whipped and slightly sweetened
- maraschino cherries

Moisten bread slices in mixture of milk, sugar, and vanilla. Layer 4 slices in a decorative serving bowl. Cover with a layer of applesauce and a layer of whipped cream. Repeat layers once. Cover and refrigerate at least 6 hours or overnight. Garnish with maraschino cherries before serving.

Ginger Cake
Pepparkaka

Jean L. Johnson, St. Peter, Minnesota, is a "part-Norwegian" married to David, a "part-Swede." She received this recipe from her sister-in-law, Birgit Jonsson Johnson, who grew up in Kalmar, Sweden.

- 1/2 cup butter
- 1 cup sugar
- 3 eggs
- 1 teaspoon cinnamon
- 1 teaspoon ginger
- 1 teaspoon cloves
- 1-3/4 cups flour
- 1 teaspoon soda
- 2/3 cup sour cream

Beat butter and sugar until light and fluffy. Add eggs and spices. Sift flour and baking soda together. Add alternately with sour cream. Stir until well blended. Pour into deep round cake pan (or 9x5-inch loaf pan) that has been buttered

and sprinkled with bread crumbs.
Bake at 325° for 15 minutes.
Reduce heat to 250° and continue
to bake 30 minutes longer until
cake tests done. Loaf pans take
longer. Freezes well.

Apple Cake
Äppelkaka

*Justine L. Olson, Lindsborg, Kansas,
says, "I am a homemaker and have
worked as a secretary at Bethany
College for over 20 years. I enjoy all
the Swedish customs even though I
am not Swedish. My husband is, and
we have two boys that sure look like
the Swedes over in Sweden."*

1-1/2 cups sugar
  1/2 cup shortening
    2 eggs, beaten
    3 cups chopped uncooked
      apples
    1 teaspoon vanilla
1-1/2 cups flour
    1 teaspoon baking soda
    1 teaspoon cinnamon
    1 teaspoon nutmeg
  1/2 cup chopped nuts
  1/2 teaspoon salt
1-1/2 cups brown sugar, packed
    2 tablespoons milk or cream
    5 tablespoons melted butter

Mix all but last three ingredients
together and pour into greased
13x9-inch pan. Bake at 350° for 25
minutes. Remove from oven and top
with mixture of brown sugar, milk
or cream, and melted butter. Return
to oven and bake another 25 minutes. Delicious with ice cream.

Ambrosia Cake
Ambrosiatårta

*Marianne Baeckstrom is a member
of The American Swedish Historical
Museum, Philadelphia.*

    3 eggs
    1 cup sugar
    1 cup butter
    1 cup flour
  3/4 teaspoon baking powder

Beat eggs and sugar until white and
fluffy. Stir butter until creamy and
add to egg mixture. Sift together
flour and baking powder. Add to
egg mixture and stir until well
blended. Pour into 9-inch round
cake pan that has been buttered
and sprinkled with bread crumbs.
Bake at 320° for 30 minutes.

Icing:
    1 tablespoon orange juice
  1/3 cup powdered sugar
    3 tablespoons chopped
      candied orange peel or
      chopped almonds
Mix orange juice and powdered
sugar until smooth. Spread evenly
over cake and sprinkle with orange
peel or almonds.

Variation: Rosemary Plapp
sprinkles 1/4 cup of rum on the
cake after cooling, before frosting.

Chocolate Roll
Rulltårta

Inger Lofgren, Edina, Minnesota, says this cake "would be part of a traditional Swedish coffee table."

3 eggs
3/4 cup sugar
1 tablespoon flour
1/3 cup cornstarch
1 teaspoon baking powder
2 tablespoons dry cocoa
5 tablespoons soft butter
1 cup powdered sugar
1 egg yolk
1 teaspoon vanilla

Beat the eggs with the sugar until light yellow and fluffy. In a separate bowl, mix the flour, cornstarch, baking powder, and cocoa. Stir into egg mixture. Pour the batter onto a well-greased foil-lined cookie sheet and spread evenly. Bake at 400-425° for a few minutes, until done.

Using the aluminum foil, turn the cake upside down onto a piece of paper sprinkled with sugar. Let the cake cool, covered with a towel. Mix the butter, powdered sugar, egg yolk, and vanilla and spread evenly on cake when cool. Roll cake lengthwise with the help of the foil. Wrap tightly in foil and refrigerate until ready to serve. Serves 8-10.

Editor's note: Swedish cocoa comes from Africa, American cocoa from South America. They are somewhat different in color as well as flavor. Swedish cocoa is darker. American cocoa used with baking powder comes out gray in cookies or cake; with soda the color is closer to the appearance of Swedish cocoa.

Glögg Cake
Glöggkaka

June Forsberg Moniz, Montclair, New Jersey "I use this instead of fruitcake at holiday time. It can be stored in the refrigerator or frozen. Small loaves make an ideal and unique gift. After you make glögg (a fruit and liquor punch), cool the drained fruit, remove rinds from the fruit and remove solid spices (cloves, cardamom, and cinnamon sticks). Chop the whole almonds. There will be about 6 cups of glögg fruit, which I store in 2-cup containers and it can be used any time."

1-1/2 cups applesauce
1/2 cup shortening
1 cup sugar
2 cups *glögg* fruit, cooled, without solid spices or rinds
1/2 teaspoon cloves
1 teaspoon cinnamon
1 teaspoon nutmeg
1/2 teaspoon salt
2 cups bread flour
2 teaspoons baking soda
   chopped almonds

Heat applesauce. Combine shortening, sugar, and *glögg* fruit in hot applesauce. When cool add spices, salt, flour, and soda, and mix well. Add nuts. Turn into a greased and floured Bundt pan. Bake at 350° for 1 hour, or until done.

Blueberry Tart
Blåbärspaj

Irma Greenspan is a member of The American Swedish Historical Museum, Philadelphia

      2 cups flour
    10 tablespoons butter
      3 tablespoons sugar
      1 egg yolk
1 to 2 tablespoons cold water
Filling:
      3 eggs
      6 tablespoons powdered
           sugar
  1/2 cup whipping cream
      1 pint fresh or frozen
           blueberries, thawed

Mix flour, butter, sugar, and egg yolk, using a pastry blender or fork. Add water gradually, using just enough to make a dough that is quite firm. Refrigerate at least 2 hours. Roll tart pastry into a circle about 1/4-inch thick. Place on a 12-inch tart pan. Shape edges at least one inch high to hold filling. Prick the bottom with a fork and bake at 375° for 10 minutes.

Beat eggs, powdered sugar and cream and pour into tart shell. Add blueberries and bake about 45 minutes at 375° until firm. Additional cream may be whipped to serve on top. Serves 16.

Wreath Cake
Mandelringstårta

Delores A. Meyers, St. Louis Park, Minnesota, won the 1980 International Hall of Fame award for cake decorating. That year she also received a personal gold medal from the King of Sweden for her volunteer work with Scandinavian groups.
"I have worked at Maid of Scandinavia for 26 years, I teach cake decorating and professional candy classes. For 17 years I have written a newspaper column, 'Delores Decorates.' Both of my parents are Swedish."

       3 cups almond paste
1-1/2 cups granulated sugar
       4 egg whites, slightly beaten

Break almond paste into small chunks. Add sugar and egg whites. Mix ingredients thoroughly with a electric mixer. Fill a 12- or 14-inch pastry bag equipped with either a 6P or 6CS pastry tube with the paste mixture. Spray *krans kaka* rings (available at Scandinavian specialty shops) with non-stick cooking spray and fill with paste mixture. Bake at 300° for 20 minutes or until surface is golden in color. Remove rings when cold. Nine of the 18 rings can be baked at a time.

Icing:

> 1 **egg white**
> **powdered sugar**
> 3 to 4 **drops vinegar**

To make icing, beat egg white until it holds its shape. Add powdered sugar until icing holds its shape. Add vinegar, making sure that icing continues to hold its shape. Place in decorating bag with #2 tube. Starting with the largest ring, place it on a cardboard circle with doily and add a dab of icing in 3 spots on top of the ring. Place the next ring on top, join with dabs of icing, and continue until all rings are placed together. Add flowers, a crown, flags, or other decorations fitting for the occasion.

To serve, give top ring to bride and groom, who break it for themselves and they in turn break the next few rings into 2-inch pieces to be served to guests. An 18-ring cake will serve 75 people.

Editor's note: Lilly Setterdahl of East Moline, Illinois, reports that in Sweden the various-sized rings are formed on baking sheets rather than in ring forms.

Crispy Apple Pie
Frasig Äppelkaka

Jane Anderson, New Brighton, Minnesota, is a Swedish teacher who, along with her husband, lived and studied in Sweden four years in the 1960s. "My husband is an ophthalmologist who traces his entire family directly to Sweden. It was through his enthusiasm that I discovered that my ancestors came not only from Lebanon, but also from Sweden via a great-grandfather!

"This is a modern version of an old Swedish favorite given to me by a young lady in Sweden who helped care for our two children who were born there. Quick and easy, it is ideal for inviting friends in to 'fika' (drink coffee and chat)."

> 6 to 8 **tart apples**
> 1 **tablespoon sugar**
> 1/2 **cup water (or slightly less if apples are very juicy)**
> 1/2 **cup butter or margarine, slightly softened**
> 1 **cup sugar**
> 1 **cup unsifted flour**

Peel and core apples. Slice thinly into 9-inch pie plate. Sprinkle with 1 tablespoon sugar and pour water over apples. Cut slightly softened butter into 1 cup sugar and flour which have been mixed together. Shape dough with fingers into a small round pieces the size of a quarter about 1/8 to 1/4-inch thick. Place dough pieces on top of apples, overlapping slightly. Continue until apples are entirely covered. Bake at 350° for 25-30 minutes. The top should be golden with a few edges beginning to darken. This Swedish "pie" may be served warm with ice cream or whipped cream, or plain. It is also excellent ice cold and can be prepared 24 hours ahead if served cold.

Variation: Sprinkle pie with cinnamon and/or a few drops of lemon juice before baking.

Million Dollar Fudge

Mamie Eisenhower

4-1/2   cups sugar
      pinch of salt
2   tablespoons butter
1   tall can evaporated milk
2   (ounces) semi-sweet chocolate
12   (ounces) German sweet chocolate
1   pint marshmallow cream
2   cups nutmeats

Boil sugar, salt, and butter for six minutes. In a large bowl, put evaporated milk, semi-sweet chocolate, German sweet chocolate, and marshmallow cream. Pour boiling syrup over ingredients in bowl; beat until chocolate is all melted. Stir in nutmeats. Pour into pan. Let stand a few hours before cutting. Store in a tin box.

Photo, Joan Liffring-Zug Bourret

Luncheon for Mamie Eisenhower, third from left, Cedar Rapids, Iowa, 1958. She always wore bangs.

Annie's Swedish Coffee Party, Gammelgården Scandia, Minnesota

Relatives in Sweden and reference books provided information for a morning event featuring three courses. Coffee is served with each course. Swedish cultural history and tours are offered between courses.

1. Cardamom yeast bread, butter.
2. Three kinds of fruit-filled coffee breads and a plate of assorted Swedish cookies with three to seven varieties. Tradition calls for an odd number of cookies.
3. Almond cake with seasonal fruit and whipped cream.

Cookies

Lingonberry Cookies
Lingonkakor

Daisy Peterson Samuelson, Minneapolis, sent this recipe from her friend, Mrs. K. B. Olander. Daisy's father emigrated from Langlet, in Mora, Sweden, with his parents in 1882, and her mother was born here of Swedish parents. Daisy married Hållbus Erick Samuelson who emigrated from Mora, Sweden, in 1929. (His mother was a model in 1892 for two of Anders Zorn's paintings. One hangs in the courthouse in Mora. The other one is in Hälsinglands Museum in Hudiksvall.) In February 1976, Daisy served as the first wreath girl for the Vassaloppet, *a cross country ski race, in Mora, Minnesota. She has a beautiful costume over 100 years old from Mora.*

```
 1    cup butter
      scant 1/2 cup sugar
 1    teaspoon vanilla
 2-1/4 cups flour
      lingonberry jam
 2    cups powdered sugar
      vanilla sugar or vanilla to
         taste
      water
```

Cream together butter and sugar. Add vanilla and flour, mixing well. Divide dough into four pieces and roll each the length of a cookie sheet, about 1-inch in width. Flatten slightly. Bake at 325° for 12-15 minutes. Immediately brush with lingonberry jam and spread with glaze made by mixing powdered sugar and vanilla sugar or vanilla with water until of spreading consistency. Cut diagonally while still warm.

Variation: Use raspberry jam or strained cranberry sauce instead of lingonberry jam.

One-Two-Three Cookies
Ett, Två, Tre Kakor

Sara Requist, Storm Lake, Iowa, says, "I was just a little girl, but my grandmother taught my three older brothers how to make these easy cookies, and they taught me. I am a fifth-generation American-born Swede."

```
1/2   cup brown sugar
 1    cup butter or margarine
1-1/2 cups flour
```

Cream sugar and butter or margarine. Add flour. Refrigerate for 1 hour. Form dough into balls and press down with a fork or bottom of a plastic spool that sewing thread comes on. Bake at 350° for 8-10 minutes to a golden brown.

Ginger Cookies
Pepparkakor

Dorothy Fransen Liljegren, Rock Island, Illinois, is a graduate of Augustana College and is interested in the Swedish ancestry of her parents. Each year for 5 years she has baked one hundred dozen pepparkakor *for the Bettendorf, Iowa, International Festival.*

```
    1  cup butter
1-1/2  cups sugar, sifted
    1  tablespoon syrup
    1  large egg
    1  teaspoon baking soda
    2  teaspoons cinnamon
    2  teaspoons ginger
    1  scant teaspoon cloves
2-1/2  cups sifted white flour
```

Cream together butter, sugar and syrup until very smooth. Add egg and beat into batter. Stir in baking soda, cinnamon, ginger, and cloves. Fold into flour. Add more flour if necessary to make batter easy to handle without sticking to fingers or cookie press.

Using the bar design of a cookie press, press out several long strips of batter on ungreased cookie sheets. Bake in a pre-heated 350° oven for 7 minutes. Strips will be a medium brown. Remove from oven and let rest for 1 minute; cut into 2-inch pieces. When cool, remove to brown paper. Store in air-tight containers. Makes 7-8 dozen bars.

Butter Rings
Smörringar

Lillie M. Harrison, Minneapolis, says, "I have always enjoyed the Swedish traditions and recipes. I am a first generation American. These were special cookies that my mother made each Christmas, and everyone enjoyed them with a cup of Swedish coffee."

```
    1  cup butter or margarine
  1/2  cup sugar
    1  egg yolk, beaten
  1/2  cup milk
  1/4  teaspoon almond flavoring
  1/2  teaspoon baking powder
  1/4  teaspoon salt
2-1/4  cups flour, divided
```

Cream butter and sugar. Add egg yolk, milk, and flavoring and mix. Sift together baking powder, salt, and 2 cups of flour and add to above mixture. Add as much of remaining 1/4 cup of flour as needed to make the dough easy to handle. Roll into 10-inch strips about 3/16-inch in diameter. Shape each strip into a pretzel and press flat in granulated sugar. Place on ungreased cookie sheet, sugar side up. Bake at 375° for 7-8 minutes.

Sugar Wreaths
Sockerringar

Jenny Johnson, Minneapolis

1/2 pound butter
3/4 cup sugar
2 eggs
3-1/2 cups flour, divided
2 teaspoons ammonium carbonate crystals, crushed to fine powder
1/4 teaspoon salt
2 teaspoons cardamom
6 tablespoons cream
1 egg, whipped
1 cup pearl sugar

Cream butter, sugar, and eggs until light and fluffy. Mix 2-1/4 cups flour with ammonium carbonate crystals, salt, and cardamom, and add this to the above mixture alternatively with the cream. Using remaining flour, knead dough on board. Roll into little-finger thickness. Cut into 5-inch lengths and shape into wreaths. Brush with egg and dip in pearl sugar. Bake at 375° for about 12 minutes.

Vanilla Sugar
Vaniljsocker

A powdered sugar with a strong vanilla flavor is available in import stores. One teaspoon of vanilla sugar equals one teaspoon of our liquid vanilla.

Brides' Hearts
Leksandsbrudhjärtan

Gunhild Anderson, Minneapolis

1/4 pound butter or margarine
1/3 cup firmly packed brown sugar
1/2 cup finely chopped blanched almonds
1 egg
1-1/3 cups flour
1/2 teaspoon ammonium carbonate crystals, crushed to fine powder
1 egg white
chopped nuts (may use pecans)
1 recipe of any basic chocolate frosting

Melt butter. Add sugar and let cool. Mix together almonds, egg, flour, and ammonium carbonate and add to butter-sugar mixture. Let rest in cool place. Roll out and cut with small heart-shaped cutter. Brush with egg white and chopped nuts. Bake at 350-375° for 8-10 minutes. When cool, make sandwiches by spreading with chocolate frosting and pressing two cookies together, nut sides out.

Ammonium Carbonate
Hjorthornssalt

Many recipes for Swedish cookies call for ammonium carbonate crystals (or baking ammonia). This is available in some drugstores, although you may have to search to find one stocking it. Ammonium carbonate comes in irregularly shaped chunks and needs to be crushed before adding it to the other ingredients.

Sand Tarts
Sandbakelser

Mrs. Donald (Dolores) Benson, Saint Edward, Nebraska, writes, "Handle very carefully — these are rich."

- 1 cup butter
- 1 scant cup sugar
- 2 egg yolks
- 2-1/2 cups pastry flour
- 1 teaspoon baking powder
  dash almond extract
- 1 cup walnuts, finely chopped

Cream first three ingredients. Add remaining ingredients and mix well. Using fingers, press a small amount of dough into a couple of Swedish *Sandbakelser* forms to test bake. Work dough up the sides of the little tartlet tins, using no more dough than necessary to cover the tins. Bake at 350° until golden brown. Cool before removing from tins. Bake remaining dough the same way, handling tarts carefully to avoid breaking. (I do not wash the tins, merely wipe well with a soft cloth.)

Editor's note: Adding walnuts is American. Swedish cooks would use ground almonds.

Cocoa Balls
Kokosbollar

Eva Busch, Uppsala, Sweden, says this uncooked cookie is her family's specialty. A medical student in Uppsala, Eva once lived in Iowa City while her husband was doing research at The University of Iowa Hospitals and Clinics.

- 1/2 cup margarine or butter
- 1/2 cup sugar
- 1 tablespoon vanilla sugar
- 2 to 4 tablespoons cocoa
- 1-1/4 cups uncooked quick oatmeal
  shredded coconut

Combine ingredients in order and blend together thoroughly. Form into small round balls. Roll each ball in shredded coconut. Chill and store in refrigerator. An additional 1/2 to 1 cup shredded coconut can go into basic mixture.

*Coffee pot watertower
Stanton, Iowa*

Coffee Fingers
Finska Pinnar

*Elisabet Heisler, is a member of
The American Swedish Historical
Museum, Philadelphia.*

- 1 cup butter
- 1/3 cup sugar
- 1/4 teaspoon almond extract
- 2-1/2 cups flour
- 1 egg, beaten
- 2 tablespoons sugar
- 15 blanched almonds, finely chopped

Cream butter and sugar together until
fluffy. Add almond extract and flour
and mix thoroughly. Chill. Roll out
to 1/2-inch thickness and cut into
2-inch strips. Brush with beaten
egg; mix together sugar and almonds,
and sprinkle on top. Bake at 325°
for 8-10 minutes, or until golden
yellow. Makes about 55 cookies.

Spritz Cookies
Spritsar

Dorothy Ossian, Stanton, Iowa

- 1 cup butter
- 1 cup sugar
- 2 egg yolks
- 2 tablespoons whipping cream
- 1 tablespoon almond extract
- 3 cups flour

Cream together butter and sugar.
Add egg yolks, cream, and almond
extract. Stir well and add flour. Be
careful not to use too much flour
or it will be hard to push through
the spritz form. Shape with spritz
cookie press on ungreased cookie
sheet and bake at 350° about 8
minutes until lightly brown.

Poor Man's Cookies
Klenäter

*Elizabeth (Mrs. Einar) Jaderborg,
Lindsborg, Kansas, found this recipe
"in a very old cookbook written in old
script in a quavering handwriting on
a yellowed piece of scrap paper."*

- 6 eggs
- 6 tablespoons sugar
- 6 tablespoons cream
- 2 cups flour
- 2 teaspoons ground cardamom seed

Beat eggs until lemon colored. Add sugar. Beat well. Add other ingredients to make a soft dough. Roll out thinly. Cut in long strips 1-1/4 inch wide; cut these strips diagonally about 3-inches long. Make a small slit at one end and draw the other end through. Fry in hot lard. Sprinkle powdered sugar through a sieve.

These cookies are delicious served with fruit sauce and a dollop of whipped cream.

Crisp Sugar Cookies
Spröda Sockerkakor

Phyllis Strand, St. Louis Park, Minnesota, member of The American Swedish Institute in Minneapolis, is a ribbon winner for her cookie and cake recipes at the Minnesota State Fair.

- 1/2 cup shortening
- 1/2 cup margarine
- 1/2 cup powdered sugar
- 1/2 cup white sugar
- 1 egg, beaten
- 2 cups plus 2 tablespoons flour
- 1/2 teaspoon salt
- 1/2 teaspoon baking soda
- 1/2 teaspoon cream of tartar
- 1/2 teaspoon vanilla

Mix together shortening and margarine. Blend sugars and add to above mixture. Add egg. Blend together flour, salt, baking soda, and cream of tartar and add to mixture. Add vanilla. Blend well.

Refrigerate overnight or for a least 2 hours. Make small balls and dip in sugar. Put on lightly greased baking sheet and press with bottom of a glass (a patterned glass is a nice variation). Bake at 350° for about 8 minutes or until edges are light tan. Makes about 8 dozen.

Variation: May decorate cookies with colored sugar before baking.

Dream Cookies
Drömmar

Marianne Baeckstrom is a member of The American Swedish Historical Museum, Philadelphia. These cookies are sometimes called "Ammonium Carbonate Cookies," for that is their special ingredient.

- 1 cup butter
- 1 cup sugar
- 1 teaspoon vanilla sugar
- 2-1/2 cups flour, sifted
- 1/2 teaspoon ammonium carbonate (available in drugstores)

Preheat oven to 300°. Cream the butter, sugar, and vanilla sugar until light and fluffy. Mix the flour and the ammonium carbonate and add to the butter-sugar mixture. Blend well. Shape the dough into small balls and place on baking sheet. Bake for 20-25 minutes, until the cookies are pale and have a cracked surface. Makes 5 dozen.

Imported Cookies
A List of Favorites

Vivian Bergquist, Bergquist Imports
Cloquet, Minnesota

Gjende — a shortbread cookie with a hint of coconut stamped with a reindeer design, was originally Norwegian. Now it is made by Swedish bakers for a Finnish company.
Mint Ballerina — mint chocolate filling between 2 shortbread cookies
Citron Cookies — shortbread cookies with lemon filling
Smultron — shortbread cookies with wild strawberry filling
Ballerina — shortbread cookies with chocolate hazelnut filling
Kung Oscar Almond Crisp — thin almond cookies with almond slices, ideal with ice cream or a quick cup of coffee
Kung Oscar Pepperkaker — thin gingerbread cookies, a Scandinavian staple, but also great with cheese
Singoalla Citron-lime — shortbread cookies with lemon/lime jelly cream center
Ballerina — Apelsin/chocolate shortbread cookies with a chocolate-orange cream filling

Swedish Proverb

He who cannot kindle a fire
cannot love.

Index of Recipes

Cookies

Photo, Jim Turner

*Decorative Christmas sheaves
(julkärve) of wheat are offered by
the Swedish Folk Dancers in
Lindsborg, Kansas, at holiday time.
In Sweden, wheat is given to the
birds.*

*Christmas tile created by Bergquist
Imports, Cloquet, Minnesota*

Swedish Table Prayer

*I Jesu namn till bords vi går
välsigna Gud den mat vi får.*

In Jesus' name to the table we go;
bless, God, the food we get.

Moving Rock

Wood carving by Gunnar Svensson, Småland, Sweden
The American Swedish Institute, Minneapolis

A hard-working farmer is clearing stones from a field. Svensson's carvings document the ways of the old Swedish agricultural society. There is a long history of woodcarving in Scandinavia dating back to Viking times. Eventually woodcarving developed into a folk art used to make figures of human and animal forms, including the Dala horse, the unofficial symbol of Sweden.

Books by Mail (prices subject to change)
www.penfieldbooks.com   Email: penfield@penfieldbooks.com
Penfield Books, 215 Brown Street, Iowa City, Iowa 52245
Shipping: $5.95; two titles $7.97

$14.95 *Swedish Touches: Recipes and Traditions* (this book)
$14.95 *Sweden's Regional Recipes* compiled by Diana Johnson Kia
$10.95 *Splendid Swedish Recipes* (a mini-cookbook, 3 1/2 x5", postpaid)
$10.95 *Swedish Proverbs* collected by Joanne Asala
$16.95 *The Autobiography of Carl Larsson: Sweden's Most Beloved Artist*
$19.95 *Swedish Folkart* by Diane Edwards
Four titles by Selma Lagerlöf
$18.95 *Gösta Berling's Saga*
$16.95 *Wonderful Adventures of Nils*
        and *The Further Adventures of Nils Holgersson* (two books in one)
$12.95 *Memories of Mårbacka* (autobiographical)
$10.95 *Selma Lagerlöf's Words of Love and Wisdom*
$ 2.50 Catalog of all titles, includes Carl Larsson art books

Design by Karen Jenson